Soul Music
Discover Your Personality Type so YOU can lead a life of Happiness and Success

Awen Finn

Studio 8 Publishing

SYDNEY

Copyright © 2016 by Awen Finn

All Rights Reserved.

Studio 8 Publishing
Sydney
www.readmysongreadmysoul.com

Editor: Christine, BookEditingServices.com Cover design: Derek Murphy, Creativindie. Photo of Awen Finn: Marcus Walters Photographer

Quote from Paramahansa Yogananda has been reprinted by permission from the writings of Paramahansa Yogananda, Self-Realization Fellowship, Los Angeles, USA.

No part of this publication may be reproduced or transmitted in any form or by any means, electronic, photographic or mechanical, including recording, photocopying for public or private use, or by any information storage and retrieval system or transmitted without the prior written permission of the author, except where permitted by law.

Disclaimer: The author of this book does not dispense medical, legal or professional advice or prescribe any strategy or treatment for physical, emotional, or medical problems without the advice of a physician or a professional. This information was written out of personal experience for informational and entertainment purposes only. You are responsible for your own actions in the event that you use any information found in this book.

The names and identifying details of individuals have been changed for confidentiality purposes. The author of this book does not intend to be in any way prejudicial to the honor and reputation of the song writers, composers, musicians, and bands mentioned in this book. No song lyrics appear in this book and no formal analysis of song lyrics appear in this book.

Song Read ™

Soul Music/Awen Finn. -- 1st ed.
ISBN: 9780994167255

By the same author
Read my Song, Read my Heart, Read my Soul
How to Beat Criticism and Feel Good

CLAIM YOUR FREE BONUS GIFTS TODAY!

As a big thank you for buying and reading this book, I'd like to give you some great bonus gifts to help you on your journey to self-discovery.
So go ahead now and visit the link below to access all of your resources

http://readmysongreadmysoul.com

Here's just a peek at what you'll receive when you visit this link:
FREE Book chapters from Read my Song, Read my Heart, Read my Soul
FREE Beginners Guided meditation
FREE Competitions
You can access all this and more when you visit:
http://readmysongreadmysoul.com

For my Father in heaven, Thomas,
And his favorite song
"The Power of Love" performed by Jennifer Rush
All My Love

"I am the Cosmic Ocean of sound and the little wave of the body vibration in it."

—PARAMAHANSA YOGANANDA

Praise for
Soul Music

Here are what some of my clients have to say about their Song Read:

"I am extremely blown away by this response! You are spot on with everything! Especially with the last paragraph, most of my favorite songs have the whole band singing together. Reading through this I defiantly learned some things about myself. Thank you!"

"That was a pretty cool description of me and what and who I am. On a 1-10 scale I'd give it 9.2"

"Thank you so very much, Awen. I agree my soul is talking to me and telling me what it needs. I'll need to be a lot more successful in life (financially) as I completely love nature. In my mind I know exactly what I want and where to live and also what I need from life. Again burdened by finances. But I know one day I will succeed."

"Your interpretation is very accurate. I was 12 when I first heard this song; the year it was released in 1991."

"Thank you for your reading of my favorite song. It is all very true. I am a romantic and gentlemanly person. I love the harp, it is a very special instrument for me. It was a favorite song of my old Art Teacher, Stanley. He gave me a copy of the music, and I played the song at his funeral on the Grand Piano at St George's Cathedral a few years ago. This first verse I played quite joyfully and boisterously, and the second verse I played very softly in a ghostly manner. I think it was effective. I think that the theme of the song is rather positive, that the meaning and the most important thing in life is love."

"Nice work Awen! How do you work this out? A great gift! You're doing a good job."

"The interpretation is really lovely. I do consider myself a good communicator; I am trying to write a novel so written communication is especially important to me. I also believe I have qualities of a healer; I'm quite sensitive and empathetic to what's happening even if it isn't initially clear. I'm vegetarian and have a great love of animals and am constantly getting suckered into donating to charities when I barely have enough for myself! I guess I am a "swayer" when it comes to music and I do feel closer to "the source" when listening to music I love. Thank you again for taking the time to do an interpretation, I found it very interesting."

"That was a really interesting interpretation of my character. I must say it was pretty accurate. I look forward to reading your book."

"Thank you, Awen. I can't believe you haven't met me. Have you been Facebook stalking me? No I'm joking; I know you haven't because there was one thing there that was definitely incorrect; I have small shoulders that are rolled forward. Unfortunately I do hunch forward somewhat. However when I imagine myself, I think I have square shoulders too! All the best for your books and I will be recommending you to my friends."

"Your interpretation is so true and pretty much sums me up to a tee :)"

"Just read my reading on my song. Scary. Ha but so true. I am already a mother to five kids (28 -14) and it's so true I have a fantastic relationship with them all, we are sooo close and I see and hear of them every day. I am always there when they need me and I know when to leave them to it. Also, it was correct about friends, I get on great with a lot of people but I prefer only to keep a few close to me. These are friends I've known for over 20 years and they have never let me down. I was impressed how close you read me from just a song but it certainly made me smile."

"Being that the analysis was quite favorable/flattering - it's not likely that I'm going to reject your summary, right?! But, I have to say, you DID hit the nail on the head quite a few times... It's hardly cheating now that you've already provided your analysis, but just for you own satisfaction, I can confirm a few things that you have mentioned, if you're interested!" –*Joshua sent in a whopping five pages of feedback. Turn to "The Shadow" Song Read to read his full feedback...*

CONTENTS

Introduction 1
   How to use this book 1
"A Day in The Life" performed by The Beatles 3
"A Forest" performed by The Cure 7
"Ah! Sweet Mystery of Life" sung by Bing Crosby 11
"Best of You" performed by Foo Fighters 15
"Closer To The Edge" performed by 30 Seconds To Mars 19
"Dance with my Father" performed by Luther Vandross 23
"Dearest" performed by The Black Keys 25
"Drive All Night" performed by Bruce Springsteen 29
"Fast Car" performed by Tracey Chapman 33
"Gone Away" performed by The Offspring 37
"Helplessness Blues" performed by Fleet Foxes 41
"Hey Brother" performed by Avicii 45
"Hummer" performed by Smashing Pumpkins 47
"I Like Dreamin" performed by Kenny Nolan 51
"I'm Yours" performed by Jason Mraz 55
"Imagine" performed by John Lennon 59
"Islands in the Stream" performed by Kenny Rogers and Dolly Parton 63
"Keep on Keeping on" performed by The Redskins 67
"Kick Start My Heart" performed by Motley Crue 71
"King of Pain" performed by The Police 75
"Kiss The Girl" performed by Chameleon Circuit 79
"Lakehouse" performed by Of Monsters and Men 81
"Lateralus" performed by Tool 85

"Life Won't Wait" performed by Ozzy Osborne 89

"Like A Prayer" performed by Madonna 93

"Losing My Religion" performed by R.E.M 97

"Love Bites" performed by Def Leppard 101

"Marry You" performed by Bruno Mars 105

"Miserere Mei, Deus" Composed by Gregorio Allegri, performed by The Choir of New College, Oxford 107

"Moments of Pleasure" performed by Kate Bush 111

"Nellie the Elephant" performed by Toy Dolls 115

"Nights in White Satin" performed by The Moody Blues 119

"Nothingness" performed by Living Colour 121

"Nutshell" performed by Alice in Chains 125

"Oh, What a Night" performed by The Four Seasons 127

"One" performed by Metallica 131

"One Tree Hill" performed by U2 135

"Safe and Sound" performed by Taylor Swift 139

"Save Tonight" performed by Eagle Eye Cherry 143

"Scarborough Fair" performed by Per-Olov-Kindgren (and Simon and Garfunkel) 147

"Shine On You Crazy Diamond" performed by Pink Floyd 151

"Silent Lucidity" performed by Queensryche 155

"Sky Blue" performed by Peter Gabriel 157

"So Afraid" performed by Fleetwood Mac and Lindsey Buckingham 161

"Southern Sun" performed by Boy and Bear 165

"Standing Outside a Broken Phone Booth with Money in my Hand" performed by Primitive Radio Gods 169

"Straight to You" performed by Nick Cave and The Bad Seeds 173

"The Burning of Rome" performed by Virgin Steele 177

"The Dead Heart" performed by Midnight Oil 181

"The Death of Me" performed by City and Colour 185

"The Shadow" performed by Richie Kotzen 189

"Throw Your Arms Around Me" performed by Hunters and Collectors 197

"Unchained Melody" performed by Righteous Brothers 199

"Voodoo Child" performed by Jimi Hendrix 201

"Zzyzx Road" performed by Stone Sour 205

Acknowledgments 211

Contact Awen 213

THANK YOU 215

Have you ever wondered what your favorite song says about you? 221

CHAPTER ONE

Introduction

"Who am I?"

This is one of the quintessential questions of life. For many, it is the most important question we will encounter. As human beings, we yearn to learn about ourselves at the deepest level. We continually define and redefine our ideas of who we are as we go through life, but even so, we often remain unsure if we are really being true to ourselves.

Hereditary factors and the environment – nature and nurture – both play fundamental roles in our development, yet many of us believe that we are also influenced by something bigger. But what? Song Reads can help you on your quest to find out. There appear to be special meanings in the patterns of energy, and by interpreting the energy in your favorite song, along with the energy in you, Song Reads can paint a fascinating picture of you and your potential.

We all have favorite songs; have you ever wondered what your favorite song says about you? A Song Read is an intuitive reading of the energy patterns held in your favorite song along with the energy patterns held within you as you listen to your favorite song. Song Reads reveal the secret messages deep inside your favorite song which unlock your psyche and all your potential. They are an awesome and fascinating way to discover your personality type.

Song Reads are intuitive, and just like the music itself, they speak to us on many different levels: emotionally, instinctually, intellectually, inspirationally, and on the level of the soul. If you are seeking self-discovery and self-understanding, Song Reads can help you read the signs that mark your journey.

When we are children, we hear the voice of our Soul. We have beautiful big dreams and we are aware of how special we truly are. Unfortunately, as we age, many of us become disconnected from our big dreams and our specialness, and we lose the ability to hear the voice of our soul and our connection with that which makes our heart sing. Song Reads can help us recall those things in life that inspire us, as well as reconnect with our innate and unique talents and abilities.

We are often brought up to not know and understand ourselves deeply. The insight gleaned from Song Reads can help assure us of our specialness and guide us in our quest for understanding. Song Reads can enlighten us about our special skills and talents. As we recall the things in life which inspire us and find avenues to practice them in the outside world, we become happier. If, like me, you are looking for direction, Song Reads can help you find it. Song Reads can illuminate our current situation and confirm what our own intuition is already telling us. For many, Song Reads provide something deeper, a way to re-establish the connection with our Soul and to feel connected to the entire cosmos. Last but not least, Song Reads are also wonderful, good-old-fashioned entertainment!

In these hectic times, it can be difficult to feel connected to the world around us. But when we reconnect to that which is special and unique within us, we become happier and more connected to the world we live in. Everyone has the power to be greater than they are—more soul connected, more creative, and more loving. Song Reads can help remind us of our greatest potentials and help us find avenues to honour and express our authentic selves.

I love intuiting Song Reads because each Song Read and each person is a new mystery to explore. These Song Reads uncover the fascinating mystery of you.

There is abundant good news in Song Reads that reminds us of many attractive qualities within ourselves. Some of these qualities we are aware of and others we have overlooked. We are able to see the beauty of ourselves. We also have contradiction within us and so Song Reads can touch on qualities we find less desirable and perhaps may benefit from improvement. Subtly Song Reads can also refer to our pain and the wounds we have suffered during our lives. We are complex individuals and no matter how a Song Read plays out we can easily glean the specialness of the individual soul embraced within the lines of a Song Read.

I want to linger a while with the theme of pain and wounds. Some of us journey through life with little suffering and an easy ability to overcome painful episodes. Conversely, many of us become unhinged by our pain and fall under its spell. We mask our wounds and hope nobody will notice our flaws. The pain rules our lives. The pain has power over us. And as luck would have it we are usually unaware that this is happening. Our pain can define us and we may lead our lives habitually deflecting the pain and desperately pretending that it isn't there. It hurts.

If this is the case for you and the time has arrived to unravel the pain and the types of pain you experience or have experienced these Song Reads are for you also. Song Reads can be an opportunity to bring your pain into the light, reconcile your heartache and empower you to make new choices which can help you lead a happier and more fulfilling life.

Song Reads have helped me enormously in this way. They have given me clarity and direction in life. They have highlighted my pain and wounds and most importantly suggested the solution from my pain and distress. The secret message in my own favorite song, "This is the Sea," performed by The Waterboys, conveys moving into the spiritual life. This message about The Spiritual life is the solution for me. It is the solution to the pain and the solution to the distress I felt. We have unique paths to follow and so I don't recommend that the spiritual realm is the key for everyone. The solution to make life happier for you may be spending more time in the great outdoors and connecting with nature or perhaps spending more time alone for reflection. We are unique. We have different pains, wounds, strengths and weaknesses; Song Reads will highlight these.

Fortunately, I followed the guidance from within my own Song Read and I started to enquire and learn about spirituality. Over the years I healed my wounds, changed my career and more importantly found great joy and peace through the practice of meditation. My favorite song guided me home! Home for me is the spiritual life and I only dreamt of venturing into this realm with the guidance from my own Song Read.

I can't promise that this will happen for you, but if you are open, desire some answers and are ready to consider change then a Song Read can be a good place to start.

To demonstrate how the subject of pain may be intuited in a Song Read, let's look at a song that has special meaning for me—"Mayonnaise," performed by Smashing Pumpkins. I intuited this Song Read for a client a few years ago. I had never heard the song before and I was immediately drawn to it. It is the loud sound from the music which is a magnet for my own energy. It is easily my favorite new song, and if I had been aware of this song when I compiled my favorite 12 songs, I have no doubt that it would land in second or third place out of all of my favorite songs. This means that the contents of this particular Song Read will be significant to me. You can read the full version of this Song Read in my book *'Read My Song, Read My Heart, Read My Soul'* and here is an extract to demonstrate how the theme of pain is revealed:

"Like many of us, you have some wounds. And you want to let go and let these wounds heal. But you try to impose your will on the

world. This blurs your vision, and prevents you from taking into consideration all points of view. I sense anger and hurt. The lyrics have meaning for you. You have probably been hurt in the past and you don't quite understand why. There are energetic tears in your eyes while I am intuiting this Song Read for you. Your pain and hurt are coming through. Time, forgiveness, openness and guidance will be your allies. These lyrics seem to express perfectly, beautifully, poetically, seriously, hurtfully, truthfully what pain can do to us. Thankfully we come out of our pain."

In the actual Song Read, these sentences are strung out throughout the whole reading; they do not appear as a condensed paragraph. When we read the above paragraph, it is clear that the subject of pain is being discussed. But if this paragraph is broken into individual sentences and distributed throughout the Song Read, it is more difficult to see the weight of this subject of pain. Song Reads are subtle; we have to be prepared to piece together these subtleties. Also if a client was to receive relentless information about their pain in a Song Read, it may be a shock and undue focus may be the result. So this is the reason the message is threaded throughout the entire Song Read.

How has pain played out in my own life? I'll tell you a story and we'll end on a cliff-hanger. As you read this story, remember the Song Reads at play here, with one Song Read ("Mayonaise") raising the issue of pain and a second Song Read ("This is The Sea") providing the guidance and solution from this pain.

I remember myself at the age of twelve vividly. It is the year that most profoundly affected my life for two distinct reasons—one for good and the other for bad.

Music first appeared for me at the age of twelve when I discovered my fifth favorite song, "Dreams" by Fleetwood Mac. As a young and impressionable twelve-year-old, I would dream I was living beside the beach in California, (which, to a young British girl sporting a Stevie Nick's hairdo, seemed to be the perfect landscape full of potential.)

Music ignited my imagination and gave me hope, which is just as well because I was about to start leaning heavily on the gifts of music.

Also when I was twelve, my father and tw0 of my older siblings arrived home from a long overdue vacation spending time with my father's family and relatives overseas. As fate would have it, my father didn't arrive home empty handed; he arrived home with his new best friend, alcohol.

My father had discovered the comforts of beer and an occasional whiskey. My Father didn't drink a lot - he wasn't able to. He was exceptionally slim of build and most probably allergic to alcohol. So with just one drink he transformed from 'Dr Jekyll' into 'Mr Hyde,' with two drinks the result was havoc, devastating condemnation and damage.

My father is like many of us who turn to vices to ease our pain; we try cigarettes, alcohol, drugs and binge eating to help us cope. And I guess if we're really lucky, sex addiction is our preferred method to hide from our own inner turmoil and from ourselves.

As a twelve-year-old, my life went into upheaval. My mother worked weekend nights and slept during the days while my Dad caused mayhem. On most weekends, one sibling, (whoever was unlucky that day, I guess) would be singled out, severely criticized, brutally belittled, given a savage dressing down and blasted with harsh fault finding. The reprimand was vicious. Like clockwork, there was only one sad conclusion to this ferocious reprove and destruction. The grand finale where the unlucky victim was literally thrown out of the house and told to "Go." The mortified victim was shamed, humiliated and made to feel like a scabby dog. The uproar was devastating. It was awful. We were left with no doubt whatsoever about our badness and the general sense of distaste we emanated. We were expelled from the family, expunged. We were not wanted. Sadly, we always returned, only to relive the hell the following week.

My ears had become finely tuned to the first signs of chaos and distress in the household. My anxiety and nervousness levels soared. I walked around with a bad feeling all weekend, hoping I wasn't selected for punishment and trying to stay out of trouble. The emotional abuse was difficult to cope with. I felt unloved and unwanted. I also felt dirty and desperately shamed and humiliated. Along with this, I also felt aggressive. When it was my turn to be in the firing line, I mirrored my father and launched verbal comebacks, which only antagonized my father more. The 'throwing-out ceremony' affected me intensely. I attempted to run away a few times. I was a simple girl and had no idea how to run away. My running away pack only included two items—a comb and a cardigan! I'd never heard of hitching, so I'm not sure what my plan was and needless to say, I didn't run far.

To cope, none of us cried. We tried to be strong and we didn't tell anyone the horrors that went on in our house. My best friend had no clue of my weekend turmoil. It was our little family secret. All of my brothers and sisters (there are six of us) behaved differently throughout this ordeal, some naturally more sensitive than others and some employing reason and logic to comprehend the situation. For a couple of my siblings "their protector" trait came to the fore. For me, my survival instincts predominated and I worked hard to display no fear to my father. As time progressed, we entered the era of punk rock and I adopted the dress code, with my long locks traded in for a peroxide blonde short spike hairdo. So at least I looked tough.

I swallowed my emotions and got to work building my imaginary armor out of energy. I truly believed "Gandalf" (from' Lord of The Rings') was with me and by my side. Invisibly and energetically I constructed brick walls around my aura. I felt invincible. My unsaid words to my father were, "You will not pass."

This upheaval in the house happened on a weekly, fortnightly or monthly schedule and I endured it for years. For years we all returned home several hours after our expulsion. Relief for us came at the age of eighteen when we left home to attend university or Art College.

As with all good stories, there's usually a complication. So let's introduce another chapter. Nine years after leaving home, I had arrived at the grand old age of 27, a woman of the world believing that I had sorted out and reconciled with my childhood issues. I'd been living in Australia for two years, far away from the turmoil of my youth. My mother was turning 60 and there was a big birthday celebration planned. I thought it would be fun to go home unannounced for the occasion.

I had forgotten the danger. The surprise visit didn't go as planned. I arrived home a couple of days before the big celebration, thinking it would be fun and everyone would enjoy the surprise. But the bombshell was on me. Unbelievably and shockingly, within 24 hours, my father was up to his old habits and with just a couple of drinks he unleashed verbal hell on me. We re-enacted the insults and barbs from my teenage years, culminating with us shrieking at each other from opposite sides of a tightly shut bedroom door. But the bedroom door didn't keep the demons at bay and to my horror I was evicted from the family home. Again.

I had been in England for less than 22 hours and I'd been thrown out of my home. I was appalled. I was incredulous. I felt utterly shocked. The voices inside my head screamed, *Oh no, not this again...* I was grown up. This wasn't supposed to happen, not when I'd been away for two years. I thought my father would be pleased to see me. But I was wrong. Was I really this awful? Was I really this bad? Was I really this unlovable? Even worse, the realization was dawning upon me that perhaps I may be the runt of the litter. I clamoured for my invisible armour but it had gone. I had dismantled it. I called for 'Gandalf,' but I hadn't needed his protection for so long, he'd gone to help others. All of my earlier devises to deflect the rejection and pain had long since left me. I had softened. I wasn't so tough now. I had worked hard to stuff my emotions within me, within a dark space, locked away and to deny them that I wasn't prepared for them to be unleashed and the full emotional force of my hurtful teenage years rose up and slapped me in my face and mocked me.

I stayed for the birthday celebration. Within a week, I returned to Australia. When I arrived at my apartment, I had become frozen in shock. I undressed, went to bed, curled up and didn't move for a month. I had entered the dark abyss.

So there you have it; if you have pain, a Song Read will reveal it. If you have happiness a Song Read will show it. If you desire a solution to your pain a Song Read will probably suggest it. We all have individual paths to follow in life and at various junctures the path may be straight, curvy, crooked, sunny, foggy, bright and dark and no matter which section you are travelling, if you want some reassurance, insight, guidance or perhaps some answers, consider Song Reads; they may help.

How to use this book

I hope this book encourages you to be curious and look into the secret messages held in your favorite song. Look through the contents page of this book and locate your favorite song, or a song in your top 12. If it does not appear in the list, then see if you can locate your favorite band or musician. Turn straight to that particular Song Read and see if the Song Read applies to you as well. As an example, one of the songs in this book is in my own personal top 12, "Losing My Religion," so this is the Song Read I would turn to first. It can also be fun to locate songs and bands whose music you used to like in earlier years. Do you recognize an earlier version of yourself in this Song Read? Are your friends', siblings' or partner's favorite songs here? Then why not discover these Song Reads together? If your favorite song does not appear in this book, please contact me privately to receive a personalized Song Read.

Our favorite songs in some subtle way bring each of us to heaven. Throughout these Song Reads I like to use the word Source but it is interchangeable with The Divine, God, or any words you use to ascribe to this higher power. And just as there are many different religions and avenues of spirituality o connect with Source, there also seems to be a multitude of different sounds in music to connect with Source.

Remember, we all have free will. You have free will to change your mind about things and to change the way you think. So, if you don't like an aspect of a Song Read, my advice to you is to choose to let it go and to not put your focus on that area. Take what you like and leave the rest!

In addition, these Song Reads are not the only or full version of you. We all have contradictions within us. A song, by its nature, will not cover all aspects of you, but it will tend to highlight some important themes for you or about you. This is not a full birth/personality read of you. My hunch is that your favorite three songs will give a very significant intuitive read of your profile and your favorite 12 songs will give a full intuitive read of you, your personality, preferences and psyche.

I have changed all of the names of my clients for these Song Reads to protect their privacy and I offer my very special thanks to all these pioneers for generously offering these songs to me with openness. I feel that all of these Song Reads are "good," and as we are all connected they are all relevant and ultimately helpful for everyone.

I hope you enjoy this selection of songs. Many of these song are famous and you will know them well, while others are more unusual song choices. Regardless, each Song Read brings a little piece of the equation of our specialness home to us.

And finally, consider the possibility, that perhaps we don't choose our favorite song…just maybe our favorite song chooses us.

I wish you love and joy always,

Awen

CHAPTER TWO

"A Day in The Life" performed by The Beatles

If this is your favorite song, then you are probably special in these ways:

- Genuine
- Sincere
- Loyal
- Content
- A tad mischievous
- Take life in your stride
- Have a charming laugh
- Have a good sense of humor
- Open to diversity
- Secretly drawn to the bizarre
- Desire to be aware of all facets of yourself
- Connected with your inner child
- Express and have fun
- Future orientated
- Well-regarded and liked by your peers
- Thoughtful
- See life with the potential to be an epic journey

Client: Jeff

It has been a pleasure to intuit this Song Read for you.

I interpret your deeper connection to the song in this way:

You are genuine, sincere and loyal. You have a full heart. You like the sound of John Lennon's voice and this is one of the draw cards for you. You are content. You are a tad mischievous and you have a sparkle in your eye when you smile.

You work at a relaxed pace and you take life in your stride.

Your sense of humor is coming through. You have a charming laugh and a good sense of humor.

On the whole, you are open to diversity in life. You are accepting of people who are different to you. You don't tend to judge. You take life in your stride in this way. You are accepting of many things and many people.

You are secretly drawn to the bizarre, though this is not an obvious quality within you. On the surface, you appear to be a regular personality, but you have your secret sides and these are a little more unusual. This song allows you to connect to your hidden shadow side because you desire to be in touch with all of yourself and all of the facets of you. This is a commendable quality.

If the lyrics have special meaning for you, you are aware of this.

The *'Dr Who, Tardis sound'* illustrates your connection with two things. You are connected with your inner child, the little boy within you, and your capacity to express and have fun and you acknowledge this side of yourself. You are also welcoming of the future. You live in the present day and you are expectant of good things to come with the future. You do not tend to spend too much time thinking back to the past or ruminating about the past. This is not your way, and again, this is to your credit.

One of the main connections for you is 'John Lennon.' You admire this man.

You are connected to Source. (I like to use the word Source but it is interchangeable with The Divine, God, or any words you use to ascribe to this higher power.)

You are genuinely a nice person and you are well regarded and liked by your peers.

This is a good song choice for you because it brings to light another facet of you, which isn't such an obvious dimension. But when you smile, the sparkle in your eyes expresses this facet of you. This sparkle expresses that you are comfortable and fine with the bizarre in life. You accept and appreciate it and you are accepting of the unexpected as well.

You have an orientation toward the future.

You tend to express along the lines of the concept of 'less being more.' Another words, you are not a show off. You are more of an understated kind of personality, with a lot to contribute and offer. You are thoughtful and consider what you are going to say before you speak. You are not reactionary. You tend to be steady in your personality.

Your energy field expresses as somebody who will be and works happily in a relationship of two, as in a couple relationship with giving and receiving working well with you. A relationship will suit you.

Sometimes your logical side may overtake, as it is stronger than your emotional, creative side.

You probably aren't expecting this, but meditation will suit you because it will open new worlds to you, which you are naturally accepting of and happy to bring into the bigger equation of your life. Meditation will also give to you some sense of a 'Magnum Opus' and perhaps you see life with the potential to be an epic journey and to be a *magnum opus*. You understand that life can hold this potential.

CHAPTER THREE

"A Forest" performed by The Cure

If this is your favorite song, then you are probably special in these ways:

- Able to sense the energy of spirit
- Drawn to wonder and a sense of awe
- Able to tap into expanded consciousness
- Healthy
- Drawn to the cosmos
- Attracted to locations which have vital, clean energy
- Open to higher thought and higher guidance
- Intuitive
- Open to other phenomena and other dimensions of life
- An upstanding member of the community

Client: Harry
Thank you for the opportunity to intuit this Song Read for you.
I interpret your deeper connection to this song in this way:
This song and music connects you easily to Source. (I like to use the word Source but it is interchangeable with The Divine, God, or any words you use to ascribe to this higher power.) The sounds at the beginning of the music, represent for you, Spirit raining down and talking to you. *Raining* and showering down on you. This is important

for you. What you are vitally experiencing here, when you listen to this music, is a sense of electricity. Physical and energetic electricity. This is Spirit pouring down through your crown chakra, through your body, right down through your feet and into the earth.

Clairvoyantly, there are images of outer space and rockets darting here and there.

Your heart is smiling with this sound.

This music is also allowing you to connect with a sense of wonder and a sense of awe. Beneath your consciousness, you want to connect to the atmosphere in a much bigger way. You may or may not be conscious of this. You are connecting, energetically to a larger field of energy than your own.

You are connected with Source and throughout the whole music very clear energy is showering down on you. It is as if the cheeks in your face are collecting this energy. You are drinking the energy. The energy is also going down through your body. Your energetic body is nice and balanced and clean and healthy.

The sound is the important factor for you. It gives you a touch and sensation of the cosmos.

You also probably enjoy the atmosphere of being in a forest, particularly a rainforest. There is a cleansing and a clean energy in a rainforest. Some habitats on earth embody a very clean energy, such as the land beside the sea, mountains, country fields and forests. So you are attracted to these places because of this clean energy, which matches your own energy.

Another area which is activated in you with this music is the back of the head. You are open to higher thought, intuition and higher guidance. You are aware that there is more going on in life than the physical world and you are open to other phenomena.

It may be enjoyable for you to express yourself through art.

Dawn is a wonderful time of the day for you. You would perhaps enjoy meditation.

The sound of the electric guitar really helps you feel and express other dimensions of life.

Another message coming through is to always make sure you are grounded, literally through planet earth.

You are an upstanding member of the community too!

CHAPTER FOUR

"Ah! Sweet Mystery of Life" sung by Bing Crosby

If this is your favorite song, then you are probably special in these ways:

- Possess good, old fashioned values
- Romantic
- Enjoy holding and being close to people
- An upstanding member of the community
- Respected
- like love
- Compassionate
- Forgiving
- Grateful
- Content
- Open to learning
- Polite and possess good manners
- Wise

Client: James

It has been a pleasure to intuit this Song Read for you. I had not heard this music before.

I interpret your deeper connection to this song in this way:

You possess good, old-fashioned values. You are romantic and gentlemanly. You have a warm smile and I sense you dancing with a partner and twirling your dancing partner around. This dancing helps you to express your feeling for this song.

You are connected to Source with this song and your crown chakra is beautifully connected. You enjoy the lyrics and there is a deep significance of this song for you and you are aware of this. It perhaps marks a special occasion or something along these lines.

You have a lovely, clean energy field.

Historically, there have perhaps been issues with negative judgments, criticisms and stubbornness. But this is showing up in the past along with an attachment to old details without looking at and considering the big picture. This energy is showing not in the present, it is in the past. You do not tend to be like this now.

Clairvoyantly, I see your arms holding someone and you enjoy holding and being close to people, especially your family and wife.

You are an upstanding member of the community and you are well respected. The reason you are respected is because you respect others.

You like love. You like romantic love. This is special for you. Your thoughts about love are perhaps more prevalent in you than your emotion of love. The energy in your arms is especially warm, strong and full. The arm chakras are connected to the heart chakra by meridians. So your arms are showing the aspects and gifts of the heart chakra: love, compassion, forgiveness, appreciation, gratitude and contentment. You possess these qualities.

You are now able to look back and to see how you have learned and were open to learning through the various life challenges you received. This is to your credit. So you are presenting as a good student of life!

You may perhaps enjoy reading literature and it is beneficial for you.

You are well liked, but you tend to have a narrow range of friends, whom you love very much and who love you. You possess gentlemanly qualities of politeness, generosity, good manners and etiquette.

I sense that we are not finished, so let's take a look at a different version of this song by another artist you have recommended.

"Ah! Sweet Mystery of Life" sung by Jeanette MacDonald and Nelson Eddy

This version is important for you. You become more expanded energetically and become lost in a sense of rapture. Your ajna chakra is also activated in this version. This chakra is involved with the big picture in life, wisdom and the ability to align your will with that of your higher self.

The harp is the sound of singing angels for you.

You absolutely agree with and try to be guided by the lyrics. There is bliss here for you as well.

This song has a wonderful title for you and serves as a beautiful guide and love song for you as well.

You enjoy the opera and the consuming power of love.

Client Feedback

"Dear Awen,

Thank you for your reading of my favorite song. It is all very true. I am a romantic and gentlemanly person. I love the harp; it is a very special instrument for me. It was a favorite song of my old Art Teacher, Stan. He gave me a copy of the music and I played the song at his funeral on the Grand Piano at St George's Cathedral a few years ago. This first verse I played quite joyfully and boisterously, and the second verse I played very softly in a ghostly manner. I think it was effective. I think that the theme of the song is rather positive, that the meaning and the most important thing in life is love.

Thank you for the time that you put into giving me a reading."

Sincerely,

James

CHAPTER FIVE

"Best of You" performed by Foo Fighters

If this is your favorite song, then you are probably special in these ways:

- Big hearted
- Empathetic
- Full of loving energy
- Uplift other people
- A good friend
- Optimistic
- Truthful
- Loyal
- Possess a good sense of humor
- Stable and secure
- Genuine
- In harmony with spiritual laws and spiritual thinking
- You look for the good in people
- Accepting and appreciative
- Joyful

Client: Sindari

Thank you for the opportunity to intuit this Song Read for you. I had not heard this music before.

I interpret your deeper connection to this song in this way:

You have a big heart and wonderful empathy for others. You smile through your heart and the energy goes down to your toes and up to the crown of your head. You are a wonderful person.

You are full of energy, loving energy. You easily uplift other people. You are very connected to Source. You are a good friend and you are optimistic, truthful and loyal. You have a genuine laugh and a genuine smile. The smile from your heart reaches your eyes. You also possess a good sense of humor.

This song suits your energy field well. Your energy field grows bigger and bigger under this sound. This song affects you greatly. Your energy field is also stable. You are stable and secure. You are secure in who you are. You are exceedingly genuine and you show your whole self to the world. Your thoughts are generous. The sounds in this song mostly affect your heart chakra. There are some louder crashing sounds but your energy field is not moving with the louder sounds. This is a good song choice for you, as it suits your energy very well.

You are in harmony with spiritual laws and spiritual thinking and you are open minded. The sound is great in your energy field. You feel alive. Your energy field is wonderful and you help others without perhaps realizing it. You raise others by your presence and maybe you are not aware of this. You look for the good in people and the good in situations and events.

You agree with the sentiments of the lyrics and try to live your life from these sentiments.

You are a wonderful person and have wonderful soulful qualities and possess qualities of love. You have acceptance. You appreciate easily. There is great joy in you. Your joy is secret in you. There is a sublime hidden joy in you. I'm smiling as I am intuiting this Song

Read. Go forth and just be. It gives me great pleasure to see people like you holding your ground in this world.

You truly are a lovely gem! Overwhelmingly, your heart is huge.

CHAPTER SIX

"Closer To The Edge" performed by 30 Seconds To Mars

If this is your favorite song, then you are probably special in these ways:

- Have an active brain
- Like to enjoy yourself
- Love fresh opportunities
- Intrigued by new viewpoints
- Future orientated
- Optimistic
- Open minded
- Balanced amongst the faculties of intellect, emotion and intuition
- Enjoy meeting people
- Genuine
- Respectful
- Forgiving
- Compassionate
- Empathetic
- Grateful
- Patient and tolerant

Client: Lewis

It has been a pleasure to intuit this Song Read for you. I had not heard this music before.

I interpret your deeper connection to the song in this way:

You have an active brain. You like to enjoy your life and you like the 'new.' You appreciate and are open to newness and freshness. You love fresh opportunities and new viewpoints. This intrigues you and interests you. You are 'new' in thought. This means that you are not too interested in older, traditional thought patterns. Rather, you prefer the new and you are more orientated to the future because of this. So, you are young in mind too.

You are also naturally optimistic and open minded.

You laugh easily. You know how to enjoy yourself.

You are a balanced person. You are balanced amongst the faculties of intellect, emotion and intuition. This is actually quite rare! Many people usually have a predominance of activity in one or two of these areas.

You have a nice, clean, open, warm and welcoming heart chakra. You like to meet people and you are genuine in your affections. You employ respect and, dare I say, decency.

This song energetically sits in your upper chakras from the heart chakra upwards and rests mostly in your heart chakra, shoulders and across the level of your ears. This song opens you to the qualities of your heart: forgiveness, compassion, empathy, appreciation, gratitude.

You also display patience and tolerance. You hold any criticism in check and you admit to it. When you become aware of negative critical thinking, and perhaps apologize when it comes through, this critical energy disperses very quickly. So you are similar to all of us and have some minor faults. But you are able to rectify the energy imbalance quickly. This is to your credit. You naturally prefer to be in balance.

I'm receiving an image and vision of 'Superman,' flying like a bullet, body in total alignment. This is probably how you would like to be in life. This may be an image you have—of speeding through the galaxies, unperturbed and without encountering any obstacles. There's far more space up here for new thought and freedom.

The rapid sound at the beginning of the song shows your openness to possibilities.

Your crown chakra is nicely connected with Source, though you don't tend to emphasize this area of your life. The idea of 'balance' again.

The major message is your thought processes of possibility, opportunity, fresh thought and allowing and welcoming this to come through and exist. You are a great facilitator in this way. Clairvoyantly, you are smiling when I say this and your throat chakra lights up. You are aware of this.

You also have nice, clean, open and warm energy in the palms of your hands. Our palm chakras are connected via meridians to the heart. When we are shaking someone's hand our heart chakras are meeting. There is a 'giving and receiving.' This is something that will intrigue you in life; the idea of the harmony and the balance of giving and receiving and this working in tandem and harmony. This is an area which, perhaps subconsciously, you are drawn to. You are also perhaps naturally practicing this. You have an interest in understanding this essence of giving and sharing, mutual giving and sharing. The reason you are interested in this is because it will give you an answer to the next stage of your development.

You are an optimistic, happy person, nicely connected to Source.
Of interest for you, perhaps check out the spiritual meaning associated with the shape of the triangle.

CHAPTER SEVEN

"Dance with my Father" performed by Luther Vandross

If this is your favorite song, then you are probably special in these ways:

- Gentle
- Sweet and lovely
- Devout
- Empathetic
- Sensitive
- Tactful
- Have grace
- Sincere
- Believe in fairy tales
- Appreciative and grateful
- Give and receive love easily
- Considerate and helpful
- A fortunate individual

Client: Terry
It has been a pleasure to intuit this Song Read for you. I had not heard this music before.

This is a shorter Song Read. I interpret your deeper connection to this song in this way:

You are sweet, gentle and lovely. You are wonderfully connected to Source with this song. Your whole rib cage and your heart are filled with the energy of love.

You are devout.

You are a finely tuned individual, which in this case means you possess soft sensitivities of empathy, sensitivity, tact and you have grace. Your feminine side is developed. You are sincere and have a sincere smile and sincere facial expressions to match your sincere spirit.

You believe in fairy tales.

The energy in your arms and heart is strong and full. You express the qualities of the heart: compassion, forgiveness, love, appreciation and gratitude. You give and receive love easily. You are also kind in your thoughts towards others.

Perhaps this song is autobiographical for you and your father is saying 'Hello.'

You are a great helper in life. You help people along. You are considerate and helpful to others. You have helping hands. You possibly have healing hands.

I do feel that the lyrics are true for you. You have a lot of energy and there are some energetic tears with the lyrics. There is some sadness in this song for you as well as the positive, joyful remembrance of love.

You are a fortunate individual. You have experienced a good and happy childhood and are well placed to pass this on.

Blessings.

CHAPTER EIGHT

"Dearest" performed by The Black Keys

If this is your favorite song, then you are probably special in these ways:

- Clever
- Intellectual
- Possess good, upstanding morals
- An upstanding member of the community
- Have a steady temperament
- Responsible
- Diligent
- Loyal
- Likeable
- Possess a sharing, caring nature
- A good friend
- Helpful
- Have healing ways
- Communicate clearly and easily
- Kind
- Happy

Client: Mia

I have thoroughly enjoyed intuiting this Song Read for you. I had not heard this song before.

I interpret your deeper connection to this song in this way:

You are clever. Your brain is strong and you have a good intellect and you like these lyrics. You smile easily. You are very much of the earth and you possess good, upstanding morals. You employ high virtues. You are an upstanding member of the community.

You are exceedingly steady in your temperament and are considered and controlled. You tend to operate from your thinking brain rather than from your emotions. You perform and fulfil your duties and responsibilities well and apply yourself and work diligently at the various tasks in life. You are also loyal.

You have an amicable laugh and people like you. You possess a sharing nature and you smile and care for your family and friends. You are a good friend and help people considerably. You have healing ways and contribute to the welfare of others.

There is a languid element to you. You enjoy the sound of the castanets and the sense of easy sway. In movement and dance you also sway easily. You communicate clearly and easily and you are not afraid to express your love. Verbal communication is one of your talents.

You are intellectual and kind. You are an intellectual type of person. There is a thoughtful, welcoming friend in you, who desires to help your family and friends. The music connects you to Source. There is a happy quality in you.

You are happy when you listen to this song and you like this song.

Client Feedback

"Thank you Awen,

The interpretation is really lovely.

I do consider myself a good communicator; I am trying to write a novel so written communication is especially important to me. I also believe I have qualities of a healer; I'm quite sensitive/empathetic to what's happening even if it isn't initially clear. I'm vegetarian and have a great love of animals and am constantly getting suckered into donating to charities when I barely have enough for myself! I guess I am a "swayer" when it comes to music and I do feel closer to "the source" when listening to music I love.

Thank you again for taking the time to do an interpretation, I found it very interesting.

All the best in the New Year!

Kind regards,"

Mia.

CHAPTER NINE

"Drive All Night" performed by Bruce Springsteen

If this is your favorite song, then you are probably special in these ways:

- Easy going
- Mellow
- Romantic
- Take everything in your stride
- Serious
- Sincere
- See the good in people
- Possess an inner smile
- Have an introverted personality
- Well able to smile through your eyes and through your heart

Client: Adam

It has been a pleasure to intuit this Song Read for you. I had not heard this music before.

I interpret your deeper connection to the song in this way:

You are an easygoing and mellow individual. You have a romantic bent. You take everything in your stride and handle events as they come.

You are both serious and sincere. You have the ability to see the good in people and the good in events which happen to you and around you.

You possess an inner smile. You are an unassuming individual who doesn't try to grab the attention of others. You are a more retiring and introverted personality.

Your intellectual side is open and more developed than your emotional side. You have perhaps been raised to be a masculine figure and to embody the masculine characteristics of thinking and rationalizing rather than feeling and expressing. You perhaps do not express your feelings as openly as you would like to. This is an outcome of your upbringing and the era of your upbringing.

Your intellectual side pushes out and your emotional and creative side is less expressed than you would like it to be. You refrain from being expressive and demonstrative. Perhaps it may be beneficial to trust this aspect of your emotional and creative self. It seems that you want to be more expressive in this way.

The saxophone sound is important to you. You desire to fill life with the feeling of the saxophone sound. The full energy of the saxophone represents passion, longing and a lust for life along with empowerment. So perhaps consider yourself empowered with this feeling you want to express. It is as if your intellectualism is stopping you feeling your emotions because you have been brought up with a higher value placed on your intellectual attributes.

Your path is to express yourself more, both your emotions and your creativity. This will bring you great joy and satisfaction if you take the risk.

Your crown chakra is nice and open. You are nicely connected to The Divine. This song plays energetically in your upper chakras from heart up to crown.

The message is for you to search for this inner balance of Spirit, intellect and emotions. Your Spiritual side will easily assist you with your emotional side. Your emotional side desires this expression. This is a metaphorical triangle of inward balance, which you desire. This is the guidance of this song for you; to look to express, through risk and being in a safe environment, your emotions and to let your feminine side come out more.

You have a sincere inner smile and the piano is an instrument which helps you to connect to your emotions.

You enjoy the lyrics and understand the lyrics and the lyrics touch you. You enjoy the power of these lyrics.

Express the love in your heart, express the good you see in people and express your warmth. This is the guidance for you. This will help complete you.

Your heart chakra is developed and you are well able to smile through your eyes and through your heart chakra as well. Practice this smile through your heart because you add to the world when you do this.

Client Feedback

"Thank you Awen!!

I enjoyed reading the Song Read you sent me for "Drive All Night." Your interpretation is so true and pretty much sums me up to a tee :). The sensitive nature of my personality, particularly the emotional side has created many internal struggles along the way as I continue to reconcile my life with my own purpose and meaning. Thank you for bringing this to my attention again with your Song Read...You are so right...music truly is an expression of our soul..."

Adam

CHAPTER TEN

"Fast Car" performed by Tracey Chapman

If this is your favorite song, then you are probably special in these ways:

- Intuitive
- Feel deeply
- Subtle
- Gentle
- Work hard to contribute to life
- Feel empathy with the striving mass
- Enjoy dreaming
- Kind
- Sensitive to the needs of others
- Clear in your intentions
- Wish the world were a better place

Client: Kelly

I have thoroughly enjoyed intuiting this Song Read for you.

I interpret your deeper connection to the song in this way:

Gentle flow. You are open to other worlds and have strong intuition. You feel deeply. There is a touch of sadness and melancholy.

The gentle guitar riffs suit you well. There is a great deal of subtlety held within you. There is a quality of "fineness" in you. Your arms are full of love. (The arms are connected to the heart chakra via meridians.)

There is gentleness to you and a quiet quality within you. You are receiving a lot of energy with this song.

It is possible that you have had some hopeful desires which haven't come to fruition. If this is the case perhaps consider to pick yourself up, dust yourself off and give your dreams another attempt at success.

You are aware that the scenario of 'happily ever after' or, being happily settled in relationship, after the 'in love' stage has passed, is far more difficult to achieve than love stories would have us believe.

You are beautifully connected to Source; this song very much activates your crown chakra.

You work hard to contribute to life. However you perhaps may miss some signs of guidance along the way. You sometimes miss some of the signals. We can all do this, but there is help and signals around you and you perhaps are not always aware of them.

Maybe you would like to escape from your situation and at times be somewhere else. You are unsure why you feel this longing at times. You sense that there is better elsewhere. Better situations and opportunities etc. And you may find that this 'better' might be in the world of Spirit for you. It may also be helpful to ground your energy to the earth. In this way, you belong and become a part of the land which also sustains and connects us together.

You have great empathy for these lyrics and they touch you deeply. Maybe you have suffered from some rejection, which is a common theme and wound amongst us. This may be your sadness. This song may be autobiographical for you.

You like dreaming, but possibly at times you are unable to feel the internal power to manifest this dream. It is important to realise that this internal power is as much within you as it is within everybody else.

You have great empathy and understanding for the underdog in life. You desire to ease their situation and tell them that they are not alone. You feel empathy with the striving mass. You reciprocate kindness, which is a virtue you admire. You are kind.

The soft, gentle guitar riffs illustrate that you have a heart that wants to share understanding and is sensitive to the needs of others. When you trust somebody you become very close with them. You are clear in your intentions and don't have a lot of hidden motives. You are generally quite straightforward in your desires and your emotions. You don't wear masks and you don't tend to manipulate others; this is to your credit.

You wish the world were a better place for all of us.

CHAPTER ELEVEN

"Gone Away" performed by The Offspring

If this is your favorite song, then you are probably special in these ways:

- Optimistic
- Enjoy life
- Direct in your communications
- Respectable
- Independent
- Honour your word
- Trustworthy
- Have integrity
- Protective
- Dedicated and committed
- Logical and rational
- A secret romantic
- Dramatic

Client: Amy

I have thoroughly enjoyed intuiting this Song Read for you. I had not heard this song before.

I interpret your deeper connection to this song in this way:

You are optimistic. You look forward to and enjoy life. You also appear to be direct in your approach and communications with other people. You are respectable, independent and you honour your word. In this way, you are very trustworthy. This is one of your strengths.

I receive the image of somebody with square shoulders. Your shoulders are not slumped forward or round. You possess an upstanding personality. You are honest in your viewpoints. You do not wear masks and hide your thoughts. You present yourself to the world with few hidden motivations. People know where they stand with you and this provides a welcome relief for many people.

You display great strength and integrity. You also protect your friends from harm and hurtful comments. You naturally protect and look after others in a fatherly way. It is perhaps possible that you remember many incarnations born as a male. You seem to be more experienced in fathering than mothering in an historical past life sense. You are also dedicated and committed.

You enjoy the sound of the drums and the guitar. You like and appreciate the honest sound and resonance of these instruments being played together. These sounds mirror you very well. Your crown chakra is connected to Source. This song is pulling you and connecting you into your past history to some extent.

You may at times overthink issues. This can create obstacles and complications in your life. You present as someone who is happy to work with logic and your rational nature. You are talented in your mental capacity, but this approach can, sometimes prevent you from experimenting with your feeling nature.

You are a secret romantic. You are emphatic and have strength of feeling when you are passionate. You feel alive when you are passionate about something and you enjoy the dramatic element of this.

You may at times be timid to express your feelings, particularly your feelings of love for others. There is drama in you and you enjoy maximising the full living tragedy when you express some of the events which have happened to you. By being dramatic, these events become more alive for you.

The secret message is to experiment with and employ your courage and confidence to express vulnerability and to express your love for others. As you become more confident and practised with this, you will be pleasantly surprised with the reactions and the response you receive, which will be a mutual reciprocal sharing and vocalising of love back to you.

Client Feedback

"Thank you Awen, I can't believe you haven't met me. Have you been Facebook stalking me? No I'm joking; I know you haven't because there was one thing there that was definitely incorrect; I have small shoulders that are rolled forward. Unfortunately I do hunch forward somewhat. However when I imagine myself, I think I have square shoulders too! All the best for your books and I will be recommending you to my friends."

-Amy

CHAPTER TWELVE

"Helplessness Blues" performed by Fleet Foxes

If this is your favorite song, then you are probably special in these ways:

- Reverent
- Noble
- A balanced personality
- Communicate with clarity
- A great ambassador for humanity
- Possess high morals and sound ethics
- A free soul
- Not too attached to the material world
- Generous in your thoughts and wishes
- Like peace
- Happy in the elements of nature and weather
- Enjoy harmony
- An advocate for helpful and decisive thought
- Big hearted

Client: Noah

It has been a pleasure to intuit this Song Read for you. I had not heard this music before.

I interpret your deeper connection to this song in this way:

The world. Other cultures. You are connected to humanity. You have an understanding that we are all connected down here on planet earth, regardless of our race, sex, ethnicity and our culture. You are very connected to Source with this song. I also sense 'Hanuman' the monkey in you. (Hanuman is The Hindu Monkey God. Hanuman epitomizes devotion, service, loyalty, courage and strength.)

You are reverent, noble and sure. You possess a balanced personality. Your intellect, creativity and your emotions are nicely rounded out.

You are also very clear. You speak with clear diction and you communicate with clarity.

You uphold high virtues. You desire for all men to have a fair say and a chance to be heard and to have opportunity. You often think from the vantage point of the collective rather than from your individual view for yourself. You are a great ambassador for humanity.

You possess high morals and sound ethics. You enjoy these lyrics and they have meaning for you and you agree with the sentiment of these lyrics.

You are a free soul and perhaps desire to live with little encumbrances. You are also not too attached to the material world.

You understand that harmony in thoughts and emotions creates a lot of happiness. You are a very giving personality. You are generous in your thoughts, wishes and materially.

Your energy field is clean and unencumbered. You wish well for the world and your fellow man. You wish well for your brothers and sisters. You like peace and are guided in this way.

You are also happy in the elements of nature and weather.

You are involved with a torch of consciousness, of carrying forward a more egalitarian approach.

You enjoy harmony and you enjoy the harmony of the group collective.

In addition you are a highly regarded and finely tuned thinker, an advocate for proper, helpful and decisive thought. You are an advocate of the goal to bring more harmony and balance into the equation of you, us and the collective. You embrace this goal in life.

You have a big heart and you have an equally strong head. These will serve you well.

CHAPTER THIRTEEN

"Hey Brother" performed by Avicii

If this is your favorite song, then you are probably special in these ways:

- Open hearted
- Like to have fun
- Open to other realms
- Enjoy being with your friends
- Have expressive hands
- Like to hold people
- Have a sense of freedom
- Upbeat, cheerful and good natured
- Possess good, strong values and ethics
- A happy Soul
- Bring joy with you into the world

Client: Kelly

It has been a pleasure to intuit this Song Read for you. I had not heard this music before.

I interpret your deeper connection to this song in this way:

You have a big, wide, open heart. You come from good roots and strong morals. You have had a good, sound upbringing. You like to have fun. You enjoy yourself and you are a little bit skittish.

I am wondering whether you like horses. You are connected to Source with this song and energetically the back of your head is activated, which shows your openness to other realms.

You possibly like the color blue. The blue in the ocean, the blue in the sky and the blue color which is found in nature and wildflowers.

You enjoy being with your friends and dancing. Your hands are expressive and you like to hold people, such as putting your hands and arms on people's shoulders. You enjoy a good 'knees up' and possibly enjoy clapping along to this music while jumping and dancing around.

The tempo of this song is a good match for you.

Again I have a vision of you being on a horse. It is highly likely that you like or have an affinity with horses. You are able to enjoy the energy and the strength of a horse. The image presenting itself is of you riding a dark chestnut colored horse with a dark mane, galloping and jogging along the water's edge. You have a sense of freedom. Wind in your hair. You enjoy your freedom.

You are an upbeat, cheerful and good natured Soul. You like to smile. You agree with the sentiment of these lyrics.

You like ideals. These give to you worthy goals and parameters for how to live your life.

You possess good, strong values and ethics.

This music and these lyrics help you to feel a sense of togetherness. What you are feeling is family unity and ultimately your higher self is expressing unity with all that is. Unity with people, nature and animals. The grand magnum opus of the unity with all that is.

You are a happy Soul and you bring joy with you into the world. This is a wonderful gift.

Client Feedback

"*Wow, thanks, there is much info here that is me.*

I really appreciate you taking the time to create this for me."
Kelly

CHAPTER FOURTEEN

"Hummer" performed by Smashing Pumpkins

If this is your favorite song, then you are probably special in these ways:

- A deep personality
- Like the obscure
- Have a secret hidden smile
- Appreciate solitude
- Unorthodox and unusual
- A happy personality
- Enjoy poetry
- Highly creative
- You may be gifted
- Gifted with your creative insights and interpretations
- Possess a deep inner innocence

Client: Oscar

I have thoroughly enjoyed intuiting this Song Read for you. I had not heard this song before.

I interpret your deeper connection to this song in this way:

This Song Read is abstract.

There is an exceptionally strong energy force and connection before we commence this Song Read. You enjoy the sound at the beginning of this song. You also enjoy the breakthrough of the electric guitar which appears with a lot of clarity. There is depth to you. You like the obscure. You are very connected to Source with this music. You are showing a secret hidden smile.

You desire to constrain your natural intellectual capabilities. Sometimes you choose to not be open. It is difficult to pick up the signals for you. There is not a lot of congestion here.

I sense you as a little boy, sitting high up in a tree looking down on the world. You are alone but you are not lonely. You are softly swinging your legs. You are unorthodox and unusual and creative.

I am now switching to a different version of this song. This is a live version and it is easier to hear the sounds. Energetically, there is more openness in you now. You are thoroughly connected to Source with this sound. You love this sound. This sound transports you. There is happiness in you. Some of the music can have an almost trance-like effect for you. You enjoy the lyrics and you enjoy the poetry of the lyrics. It is probable that the lyrics hold deep significance for you.

You are highly creative and you especially appreciate the juxtaposition of the music, poetic lyrics, the pitch and timbre of the singer's voice, rising and falling. There is a suggestion that you may be talented with visual arts and especially overlapping and merging different art forms together, such as visual arts and literature, or visual arts and music. It is to your benefit to find within yourself the courage and confidence to express your creativity. To express your creative convictions and your creative sight. Don't worry about your talent; you possess the talent and you are gifted with your creative insights and interpretations.

Your energy field is clear, but you may find it difficult to express your emotions. It is possible that you have experienced some emotional wounds and have felt hurt in the past. You perhaps have an internal conflict between your intellectual and creative faculties. It may be to your benefit to express your emotions more frequently. This will balance you. Perhaps connect with the feelings you are experiencing when you are listening to this song and try to express these feelings.

Perhaps you are a silent type.

You may be gifted and it is possible your gifts are waiting in the wings to be brought to the surface at a later stage in your life. It also may be that you have the capacity and ability to express love through visual art, writing or vocalising the essence of love.

You have a deep inner innocence hidden within you.

CHAPTER FIFTEEN

"I Like Dreamin" performed by Kenny Nolan

If this is your favorite song, then you are probably special in these ways:

- Romantic
- Subtle
- Comfortable in the company of a group
- Generous
- See the good in others
- Imaginative
- Have a good sense of humor
- Respected and respectful of others
- Honest
- Appreciate life's blessings
- Easily flow with life's beneficial, helpful, spiritual energies
- Intuitive
- Enjoy sharing love and giving love
- Open to higher guidance
- A great ambassador for hope

Client: Jonathan

It has been a pleasure to intuit this Song Read for you. I had not heard this music before.

I interpret your deeper connection to this song in this way:

You are a romantic! You are also soft and subtle. You enjoy holding people and you are comfortable in the company of a group. You are generous and you easily see the good in others. This song connects you to Source.

Your imagination is alive and vivid and you have good wishes for the world and for your loved ones. You also have a great sense of humor.

You are happy in a family and you are a good father and aspire to be a good father. It is to your benefit to remember that we all make mistakes parenting, so perhaps choose not to be a perfect parent.

You possess good, old fashioned, wholesome values. People respect you because you respect others.

Your energy field is clear. You are honest and you appreciate life's blessings. There is a sense of flow to you. You have the capacity to easily flow with life's beneficial, helpful, spiritual energies. You may or may not be aware that you respond to your intuition with ease. You tend to follow your intuition.

Your heart is full of love and you enjoy sharing love and giving love. To you, love is the essence of life. Your chakras that are especially activated with this song are your crown chakra and the back of your head. You are open to higher guidance. Your heart is nice and clear, light and open and your jaw line wants to naturally break into a smile!

You imagine the world being a safe, secure, sensitive place for everyone. You are naturally hopeful and express hope for the world and the people in it. You are a great ambassador for hope and seeing the best in situations and in your fellow man.

Listening to this song is a great way to start a Sunday morning!
I wish for you blessings of love.

Client Feedback

"That was a pretty cool description of me and what and who I am. On a 1-10 scale I'd give it 9.2. Have a great day"

- Jonathan

CHAPTER SIXTEEN

"I'm Yours" performed by Jason Mraz

If this is your favorite song, then you are probably special in these ways:

- Idiosyncratic
- Special
- Intuitive
- Open to the possibility of angels and fairies
- Gentle
- Act and think differently to your friends
- An enigma
- Open hearted
- Bring a lot of light through to the world
- Have a sparkle in your eye
- A happy soul
- Have a special gift
- Have inner faith

Client: Eva

I have thoroughly enjoyed intuiting this Song Read for you. I had not heard this song before.

I interpret your deeper connection to this song in this way:

The sound of the guitar strings suits you and your energy. You are idiosyncratic, special and you would like to be able to fly! You are very connected to Source with this music.

You are open and receptive to your intuition and open to the possibility of angels and fairies.

You assert your personality onto the world in a gentle, idiosyncratic way.

There is an image of a beaded necklace. A string of beads. It is similar to a *mala*, which is a string of beads used to focus awareness in meditation or prayer. This symbolises the beginning and the end. It is wholeness and completion. You hold this within you. It is wise for you to listen to your inner voice, as this will not let you down.

You act and think differently from your friends. People see you as an enigma. This may be because you do listen to your inner voice. You perhaps do not respond, like so many of us do, from the surface and from the physical and ego perspective.

Another image for you is that of your arms rocking, again creating, similar to the necklace, a circle shape. Your arms rocking to and fro, cradling. This indicates your open heart and willingness to cradle all things, people and space in the world.

You bring a lot of light through to the world. You are exceedingly connected to Source and have a nice, open energy field.

Your vantage point is from a different perspective and space than your close peers and it doesn't really matter if they do or don't understand you, as there is mutual appreciation and the capacity to learn from each other. We all exist on different learning curves in this world.

This song suits your energy wonderfully. There is a sparkle in your eye. You skip through life and you are a happy Soul.

You can express tears of joy.

Secrets, special secrets. You sprinkle love. You like these lyrics.

"Lilt" is a special word for you.

You have a special gift of being able to sprinkle special loving offerings around you.

You have inner faith in something much bigger than yourself.

CHAPTER SEVENTEEN

"Imagine" performed by John Lennon

If this is your favorite song, then you are probably special in these ways:

- Purposeful
- Have goals to achieve
- Reverent
- Work at a deliberate and measured pace
- Serious
- Possess deep values
- A deep thinker
- Generous and kind
- Skilled with planning and strategy
- Accomplished
- Purpose is important to you
- At ease in the physical and practical realm
- Adept with finances
- Have a strong audio faculty and your sense of hearing is strong
- Peaceful
- Hopeful

Client: Charlotte

It has been a treat to intuit this Song Read for you.

I interpret the hidden messages in your favorite song and music in this way:

You are deep, purposeful and resonant. You have dreams and goals to achieve. This is such a famous song and it is difficult to take an individual person's energy from this song because of the sense of the collective within this song.

You like the sound of the piano. You are attracted to the resonance and reverence held within this piano sound. It is a deliberate and measured sound. You also possess these qualities of resonance, reverence and the ability to work at a deliberate and measured way towards your goals.

You love this song and you love the sentiment of these lyrics and agree with the values of these lyrics, like so many people do.

You present as a serious personality with deep values and you are a deep thinker too.

You are generous and kind.

You are connected to Source with this song and the color around you when you listen to this song is light green. Green is one of the energetic colors of the heart chakra. So, the sentiment of this song affects you deeply and sits with your heartfelt values.

You are deliberate in your processes and actions (as opposed to haphazard) and you can easily fulfil the necessary steps to achieve your goals. You have skills with planning and strategy. You are able to identify the correct goals for yourself, devise a strategy to achieve these goals and are prepared to spend the time to diligently perform the steps, in the correct sequence, to achieve these goals. You are accomplished and ordered in this way. You work easily in this manner.

Having purpose in the things you do is important to you.

You are connected to the element of earth and you find the physical, practical realm easy to manage, work with and cooperate with. You handle finances easily as well.

You may like to consider the option of learning about artists and their art making practises along with delving into art appreciation. Perhaps choose to enquire as to how artworks are conceived. This will allow you to become open to different processes which are available to us to fulfil our objectives. Another words our imagination works in many ways and a rounded experience of this may very well interest you and bring you pleasure. You would probably enjoy studying and comprehending this area of creativity. This will give you great scope and introduce novelty for you. If this interests you perhaps start with Picasso, (as John Lennon made some wonderful line drawings in a similar way.) Also look at Braque and the famous Renaissance painters especially Giotto for color and marvel at the back bending artwork of The Sistine Chapel.

The piano sound is the key here for you. This is what hooks you emotionally. There is pure love in the piano music for you.

You faculty and sense of hearing is strong.

You are attracted to reverence and appreciate this quality in people. Qualities of prayer, peace, hope and simplicity (we often make things more complicated than they need to be) are also here.

Client Feedback

"That was a really interesting interpretation of my character. I must say it was pretty accurate. I look forward to reading your book."

- Charlotte

CHAPTER EIGHTEEN

"Islands in the Stream" performed by Kenny Rogers and Dolly Parton

If this is your favorite song, then you are probably special in these ways:

- Beautiful in personality
- A fortunate individual
- Joyful
- Heart centered
- Possess a big, welcoming happy smile
- You are a gem!
- Have an uplifting effect upon people
- A special individual
- Express sheer love
- Happy
- Understand hidden laws and spiritual laws
- Enjoy wonder and awe
- Reciprocate, appreciate and share joy
- Enjoy the emotion of love
- Make others feel good

Client: Cindy

It has been an absolute joy to intuit this Song Read for you.

I interpret your deeper connection to the song in this way:

Some messages are being given before we commence with the Song Read. I am receiving that you are beautiful in personality. I am receiving that you are well connected to Source and your guides are here with you. There are tears of happiness and a luminous light at your ajna chakra. You are beautiful.

Spontaneous thought and guidance before Song Reads are rare. You are a very fortunate individual indeed.

On to The Song Read:

You are joyful and express tears of joy. You are a heart-centered individual. You express great joy and possess a big, welcoming happy smile. You have a wonderful clear energy field and this song expands your energy field. You are a gem!

Your presence raises many people to a higher vibration and level. You have an uplifting effect upon people and as I am intuiting this Song Read your energy field is becoming stronger. You are a special individual. You are exceedingly connected to Source. Your energy field is wide open. You express sheer love, tears of happiness. You are happy!

Your presence is a gift for many people. There are so many tears is this song. These are tears of joy. You feel an absolute sense of understanding of the hidden spiritual laws. You understand these. You enjoy 'wonder.' You enjoy 'awe.'

In regards to the way you affect others and raise others, it would be beneficial if you are in a work environment where you are able to touch as many people as possible.

It is an absolute joy interpreting this song for you.

You are a beautiful, clear, loving gem who contributes and understands reciprocity. You are able to reciprocate, appreciate and share joy.

You thoroughly enjoy the emotion of love. Expressing love, sharing love, romantic love, spiritual love, friendship love and children love. You absolutely agree with the sentiments of the lyrics and you try to implement these in your life. Manifesting this creates a goal for you and gives you direction. Love; what love is and expressing it. You express a deep, wide, sincere, encompassing genuine smile and you are beautiful.

You have the ability to make others feel good because you know how to feel good within yourself.

CHAPTER NINETEEN

"Keep on Keeping on" performed by The Redskins

If this is your favorite song, then you are probably special in these ways:

- Possess excess energy
- Spontaneous
- Like the quickness of speed
- Have fast and strong reflexes
- Have a 'nice' streak in you
- Agile
- Have a good sense of humor
- Centred and respond from a neutral stance
- Respond from a fresh and new perspective rather than from habitual past habits
- Quiet and shy
- Enjoy current events
- Deeply desire equality for all people

Client: Dean
It has been a pleasure to intuit this Song Read for you.

I interpret the hidden messages in your favorite song and music in this way:

You possess a good deal of excess energy. You are spontaneous, operating more from your gut instincts than from your rational intelligence. Your creative side is also stronger than your rational side.

You probably like karate or judo, or similar contact sports. You like speed and your reflexes are fast and strong. You have a 'nice' streak in you, which you try to keep hidden, but we all see it!

You are connected to Source with this song. You would like to have some more excitement in your life. It seems that you are fairly settled and you are surprised at how you have arrived at this place in life, (this makes me laugh, because this surprise happens to so many of us.) You were not expecting to be settled!

You have a lot of nervous energy. Playing a musical instrument would definitely suit you as this would allow you to have some release of this energy. You have a lot of energy, so you do need outlets to use this surplus energy. You have more energy than many people.

I sense you dancing 'the twist' at a very fast pace, or, 'the pogo,' at a quick pace. You are agile in your movements. You perhaps have a slim build. You also may enjoy acrobatics or stunt work.

You have a good sense of humor.

You are centred. You do not respond from either a too-emotional or a too-rational viewpoint. You tend to respond from a neutral stance. This is to your benefit. This means that you are paying attention and listening and then responding accordingly. You have an ability to respond from a fresh and new perspective rather than from habitual past habits. This is to your benefit.

At times you find it difficult to express your emotions. You can be quiet and shy.

You like current events and you enjoy discussing current events and having an opinion about these. However, it also appears that you are not as open, as you are able to be, with accepting opposing viewpoints. But you mean well and desire to see the underdog given a voice and a chance to succeed. This is important to you. This whole sense of equality among people is prevalent and important to you. You do deeply desire equality for all people. I wonder if you work with this deep sensitivity and aspiration through community services or similar outlets or volunteer in this capacity. This would be a wonderful way to share and to help bring peace and opportunity to others.

CHAPTER TWENTY

"Kick Start My Heart" performed by Motley Crue

If this is your favorite song, then you are probably special in these ways:

- Like excitement
- Enjoy having a good time
- Innocent
- Like the quickness of speed
- Possess an internal smile as well as an external smile
- When you smile you mean it
- At home with the sound of the guitar
- Forge strong friendships

Client: Anthony

Thank you for the opportunity to intuit this Song Read for you. I had not heard this music before.

I interpret your deeper connection to this song in this way:

You like excitement. You also enjoy having a good time. It seems that you are far more innocent than the image you project onto society (as is the case for many of us.) You like speed and you are presenting as a masculine personality. You really do enjoy having a good time and you are in your element when this happens.

You are balanced between your emotional, creative self and your logical, rational self, though your logical and rational side is the stronger.

You are connected to Source with this song and you have a clear energy body. Your energy field is clear and there is not a lot of congestion in your energy field. You possess an internal smile as well as an external smile. You have a very wide smile and a grin. When you smile you mean it. And once again, I am reminded that you really are a lot sweeter than you present yourself.

You may at times experience difficulty expressing your emotions and feelings. This is because you tend to live more in your head space than your heart space.

You like the sounds of the song. You enjoy the rapid sounds and the louder noisier sound. You become lost, mesmerized and engrossed in this sound. You are at home with the sound of the guitar. You enjoy the rapidness, the speed of the instruments. You must have a jolly good time listening to this track. You like the sense of 'rush' you feel listening to this music.

I'm wondering whether you have a motorbike.

Sometimes you may have a clouded vision towards the big picture view of circumstances which happen to you.

This song does not tend to speak of your inner emotional self because it dwells very much in your head space. You like this song and it is possible that a group of your mates like this song too and this style of music. You probably have forged strong friendships with the lads.

And I'm wondering whether you like to wear denim and leather clothes.

You like to become immersed in the vibe of having a good time and this is really what this song is expressing for you, having a good time.

Client Feedback

"Hi Awen,

You pretty much hit the mark with a lot of it, but then again the song says most of it. A difficult task to pick one song for me as music has been my biggest escape in my life apart from self-medicating, lol, with songs like Paul Kelly's "Deeper Water" still making a chill run down my spine every time I hear it to so many others. I have a house full of musical instruments yet I cannot play a single note (I have tried) and I rarely if ever don't have a radio playing 24/7.

Anyway cheers for the email.

Regards"

Anthony

CHAPTER TWENTY-ONE

"King of Pain" performed by The Police

If this is your favorite song, then you are probably special in these ways:

- See the bigger vision of life
- Enjoy laughing
- Clever and intelligent
- Add a different and interesting viewpoint to discussions
- Have a natural sense of rhythm within you
- Charming
- Articulate
- Easily persuade and influence others
- Have an open intuitive faculty
- Understand a breadth and depth of subjects
- Enjoy secrets, mysteries and cryptic clues
- Possess a good deal of general knowledge
- Mesmerizing
- Creative
- A Messenger

Client: Liam

I have thoroughly enjoyed intuiting this Song Read for you.

I interpret your deeper connection to the song in this way:

There is a groovy sound at the beginning of this song, emanating from the piano and the percussion. The persistence of the piano and secrets. You are inclined to naturally see the bigger vision of life. You can 'See the wood from the trees.' You perhaps disagree with how people are living and existing down here on planet Earth. You possess an expanded viewpoint.

You are a tad mischievous and enjoy laughing. You are clever and you add a different and interesting viewpoint to discussions.

At times, life can get busy for you. Busy doesn't seem to suit you. A measured pace and time to process your thoughts suit you rather than a harried busyness. You have a natural sense of groove about you and you have a natural sense of rhythm within you too.

You are clever and because you tend to see much, you may at times think you know more answers than you really do. Remember, nobody knows all the answers. The secret for you is possibly to ensure that you are around people where you can express your view points and encourage people to understand your viewpoints and also for you to accept people who think differently from you and maybe think less intelligently than you. Remember other people's opinions are also valid. It may be beneficial to become a tad less satisfied with your own cleverness and a little more open to the viewpoints of others. The views of others are still relevant and if you choose to practice acceptance of others opinions it will help you enormously and this will eventually expand your own viewpoints even further.

I sense that you are a good looking guy and you have charm as well.

Your faculty of intelligence is strong and it tends to take over your emotions. You appreciate intelligence and science.

You appreciate these lyrics. You enjoy the clever aspects and metaphors in the lyrics. You are articulate. You would possibly enjoy writing and you communicate with authority and articulateness. You also have the ability to easily persuade and influence people. Remember to use this talent wisely. Your energy field benefits as you become more conscious of your motivations; the more conscious you become that you are choosing to express a point of view for the good of all. If you have secret motivations that are only for your own good, perhaps become aware of this and choose not to express this point of view as you will encounter obstacles.

The music connects you with Source. Intuition is readily available for you if you choose to tune in and receive the signals and signs. Your faculties are clear for this to happen. You enjoy understanding a breadth and depth of subjects and there is a sense of destiny for you to comprehend more and more and more.

You possess a nice clear energy field. Your intelligence and cleverness naturally predominate. It may be to your benefit to sometimes concentrate on other less developed areas. Perhaps decide to practice humility along with your considerable intelligence.

You enjoy secrets, mysteries and cryptic clues. You possess a good deal of general knowledge as well. I receive the impression that you perform well and probably win trivia games!

There is a mesmerizing quality in you.

The longer that I am intuiting for you, your heart and the good feelings of your heart start to come through. You probably like birds (the flying kind!) Maybe the ladies as well! You are also creative, talented in English and possibly act as a Messenger at times.

I sense for you the line; 'To one whom much is given, much is expected.'

You can achieve much if you put your mind to it. At times when you feel the connection from Source, descending from your crown chakra, concentrate on this and become aware of it. This will be of benefit to you.

CHAPTER TWENTY-TWO

"Kiss The Girl" performed by Chameleon Circuit

If this is your favorite song, then you are probably special in these ways:

- Possess many sweet qualities
- Innocent
- Cherish people and objects
- A whimsical thinker
- Visual thinker
- Aware of other realms
- Intuitive
- Sincere
- Like happy endings
- You don't take life too seriously
- Possess inner peace
- Make the best out of situations
- Enjoy the absurd

Client: Heidi

I have thoroughly enjoyed intuiting this Song Read for you. I had not heard this song before.

I interpret your deeper connection to this song in this way,

You are sweet. You have an innocent aspect to you. You enjoy cherishing people and objects, which are dear and special to you. This song connects you with Source.

Your intellectual side can push out and overtake your emotional side at times. This song also plays more in your headspace than your heart space. You are perhaps a whimsical thinker.

There is a visual facet to your thinking too. With art you would probably enjoy line drawings. You appreciate the journey of a line between two points. This would amuse you greatly in a tender way. Artists to explore are Quentin Blake, John Lennon and, to some extent, Picasso.

You are aware of other realms. Your intuition is alive and kicking. You are respectful to other unusual phenomena. You do not dismiss this; you have a respect for other phenomena.

You are sincere and you have a nice smile.

People like to protect you. I receive the essence that a part of you is bird-like. Maybe you like to fly, or maybe you walk like a bird or perhaps even eat like a bird.

You like happy endings.

You enjoy the humor within these lyrics and you don't take life too seriously, which is to your benefit.

You sometimes have some reticence expressing your affections. Though you show the way you feel in your smile.

You possess an inner sense of peace. You can also make the best out of situations, even if the situation isn't to your liking.

You enjoy some absurdity in life.

You have many sweet qualities in you. You have a nice clean energy field and your presence helps the energy along. Other people are welcoming and accepting of you because you add to the energy of the group.

Lovely.

CHAPTER TWENTY-THREE

"Lakehouse" performed by Of Monsters and Men

If this is your favorite song, then you are probably special in these ways:

- Have a wonderful sense of humor
- Connect easily to your interior life
- Giving
- Grateful
- Notice the good in many situations and many people
- Possess an inner smile
- Charming
- Modest
- Likeable
- Appreciative
- Possess freedom of thought
- Open to the gifts of diversity
- <u>A</u> beautiful soul
- Trustworthy
- Enjoy people being in unison

Client: Sam

It has been an absolute treat to intuit this Song Read for you. I had not heard this music before. What a wonderful song choice!

I interpret your deeper connection to the song in this way:

You have a gentle and easy laugh. You have a wonderful sense of humor. This is quite an unusual sound. You enjoy this singer's voice because it allows you to connect to your interior life.

You work well when you are in intimate situations, as in a group of two. You are happy to share details about yourself and equally as happy to find out about other people's lives.

You have a beautiful, relaxed smile. Your energy is giving and full of gratitude and open to noticing the good in many situations and many people. This is a beautiful quality within you.

You have an inner smile, which is always switched on. You present more from your inner being than from your exterior self.

You are connected to Source. You possess an eager and expectant smile and you expect good things to happen for you and for your friends. You are charming but perhaps you are not aware of this. You are modest.

You express more of an introvert rather than an extrovert personality. People like you. Your sense of humor is beautiful, gentle, appreciative and encompassing and it is very much the first thing that came through in this Song Read. When you laugh, there is a sense of laughing at the absurd, but also appreciating the absurd at the same time.

Your mind has a sense of freedom. You possess freedom of thought. You do not tend to censor people or situations. You are open to the gifts of diversity and different viewpoints presented by other people. Even if you don't agree, you feel no need to tear people down because of their difference. You are happy to allow diverging views to exist together.

Your inner being has a beautiful sense of freedom also. Your inner being is appreciative and has a lot of gratitude. These are both high vibrational qualities.

The beginning melodies in the music almost have a feel of Anne Shirley from *Anne of Green Gables*. If you are not familiar with this character, she is always glad and says, "I am happy and I appreciate life and everything is wonderful." Anne, the character, doesn't say this in a posed and superficial way but rather in a true inner being way of appreciation. This quality of appreciation is in you too.

Fire is the element of transformation.

You are a beautiful soul and people trust you. There is inner happiness in you.

Of interest with this music is that toward the end of the song the voices aren't singing words. The singers are singing a sound joined together in unison and this works beautifully for you because often words don't have the capacity to truly express what we are feeling and thinking and sound, with its variations and subtleties, can do this. It seems that you are aware of this. When the singers join together in unison, making sound it has a meaning for you.

There is also the 'Amen' (meaning 'it is so' in Christianity) component, which you and other people desire to express as a way of thanks.

Client Feedback

"I am extremely blown away by this response! You are spot on with everything! Especially with the last paragraph, most of my favorite songs have the whole band singing together. Reading through this I defiantly learned some things about myself. Thank you!"

Sam

CHAPTER TWENTY-FOUR

"Lateralus" performed by Tool

If this is your favorite song, then you are probably special in these ways:

- Creative
- Open to inspiration
- Perceptive to nuance
- A mystic
- A cynic
- An exciting individual
- Intellectual
- Enjoy 'thinking outside of the box'
- Able to solve issues and problems
- An artist
- Fascinating
- A clever individual
- An observer
- Search for meaning

Client: Sean

I have thoroughly enjoyed intuiting this Song Read for you. I had not heard this song before.

I interpret your deeper connection to this song in this way:

These are the images which appear: Ease and flow. Being outdoors on the Road. A sense of a road trip. Unusual sounds. You are creative. You are open to inspiration. You pick up the nuances around you. There is a quality of a mystic about you. You are able to receive the finer details about people and situations.

The louder sounds seem to create some obstruction in your energy field. Sometimes you may find it hard to express your emotions.

There is a variation of sounds, depths and volume gradients within these sounds, which you appreciate. This breath is within you as well. There is a cynic in you as if you have a secret knowing, and perhaps you do. This collection of sounds is exciting and this excitement is in you too.

You are connected to Source with this music. You are open to art, creativity, abstraction and interpretation and you are open to this with your intellectual capacity. This music plays in your headspace rather than your heart space. You are enjoying the synthesis of these sounds and the meanings attributed to these sounds. This song works well with your intellect. You enjoy 'thinking outside of the box.'

You possess far-reaching intellectual capacities and you are able to solve issues and problems. You are incredibly open to the miniature nuances you encounter and the artist archetype is within you.

This is a fascinating choice of music and there is a fascinating quality to these sounds. You are fascinating too. The sounds are broad and there is plenty of scope for interpretation from you, which is wonderful. You are a clever individual. You have a nice, clean, open energy field.

You are an observer in life. You can hear, intellectualise and easily place visuals with these sounds. You prefer to process in this way rather than through your emotions. Your connection with this song is intellectual and an intellectual creative appreciation is here too.

The soothing and gentle sounds, which represent as the earlier visual and imagery of the car journey travelling across the wide-open plains, sit beautifully with you. The quest and the search for meaning sit gracefully with you. Your openness to the fine detail, the clouds in the sky, the birds up high and the shadows which the birds cast as they fly across the plains suits you well. The echo sound represents an epic quality for you. You like these lyrics, but it is the music, which pulls you. It would be nice to see you interpret visually. Visual interpretation may be exciting for you. You are an exciting individual. The creative arts suit you—drama, acting, music and absolutely visual art.

Esoteric or metaphysical study may suit and interest you.

Your mind is unusually interesting. Your mind has an enormous scope to grasp what's going on and you then proceed to process occurrences through this faculty of your mind. This is truly helpful faculty for you.

As to what you want in life, it is difficult to sense, because even though your emotions are not cut off, you choose not to express through the realm of your emotions because your intellectual capacity is so strong. You are open to intuitions as well. You are not led by your emotions, like so many others are, so it is difficult to fathom your deep, inner desires and your gut responses. This is also why you present as an observer of life.

You possess a satisfied smile. You are way ahead of your peers in intelligence.

It is good for you to laugh more as it opens up more faculties for you.

CHAPTER TWENTY-FIVE

"Life Won't Wait" performed by Ozzy Osborne

If this is your favorite song, then you are probably special in these ways:

- Enjoy the journey of life
- Appreciate the process is as important as the goal
- Have a clear mindset
- Balanced with your faculties of intelligence, emotion and intuition
- Possess a magical quality
- Have a sparkle in your eyes
- Perceptive
- There is lightness in you. You are not too serious
- Hold your own when feeling depth and passion
- Popular
- Honourable
- Have a nice sense of timing and humor
- Have leadership ability
- Amicable

Client: Grant

I have thoroughly enjoyed intuiting this Song Read for you. I had not heard this song before.

I interpret your deeper connection to this song in this way:

This is a hopeful sound. The music expresses for you a procession moving towards an end goal. You enjoy the journey of life and comprehend that the process and journey is as important as the destination goal.

This song suits your energy field well. You have a beautiful open sense of clarity in your mindset and in your energy field. You appear to be a good looking guy. You are very connected to Source. You are nicely balanced with your faculties of intelligence, emotion and intuition.

There is also a magical quality to you, which you would like to keep hidden, but it is expressed through your eyes. You possess much 'knowing' behind your eyes. You have a sparkle in your eyes. You are perceptive and understand other people quickly and easily.

There is lightness in you. This is a lightness of step, a lightness of consideration. You walk through life with lightness. You are not too serious. You don't take problems and difficulties too seriously. This is of great benefit to you.

With the deeper, more urgent sounds, you easily express the accompanying energy. Noisier sounds do not fog you, confuse you or congest you. You are able to hold your own when feeling depth and passion.

You express as balanced in your personality. You are popular. You are also honourable. This is a good choice of music for you.

I wonder if there is a secret musician in you. You enjoy the refrain in this song. This refrain is perhaps a good mantra for you. You are a 'nice' person and you have a nice sense of timing and humor. You are making me laugh as I am interpreting for you. You have within you leadership ability. People are drawn to you because you represent values and an approach to life which other people would like to adopt.

My thoughts for you are to carry on with what you are doing! I am smiling as I say this.

You are amicable.

CHAPTER TWENTY-SIX

"Like A Prayer" performed by Madonna

If this is your favorite song, then you are probably special in these ways:

- Youthful
- A happy Soul
- Innocent
- Express yourself with clarity
- Tactful and diplomatic
- Popular
- Others feel safe with you
- Possess good physical energy for sport and athletics
- Have faith
- Understand that everything happens for a reason
- Open to other realms
- Enjoy fun and spontaneity
- Unpretentious
- Authentic
- Possess a highly developed audio faculty
- A good friend

Client: Karise

It has been a pleasure to intuit this Song Read for you.

I interpret your deeper connection to the song in this way:

You have an open energy field and youthfulness about you. You have a happy and chirpy personality. You have innocence to you as well.

Your energy is clear. You speak clearly and express yourself with clarity. You don't tend to operate from hidden motivations. So you are quite direct and upfront about yourself, which is a refreshing quality.

You are a happy Soul. Skipping and chirping suit you. You are connected with Source with this song.

You possess tact and diplomacy. You are popular and people like you. People like you because you are nice, in a good way. You do not bother yourself with wounding and derogatory comments. You pay no attention with these and you do not issue these types of comments. People appreciate that you are clear, direct and easy to understand. As a consequence, others feel safe with you.

You probably enjoy dancing and perhaps you are quite talented at athletics and sport. You have good physical energy which is helpful and healthful. Exercise suits you.

You have faith and you trust in the benevolence of Spirit and Faith.

You understand that everything happens to us for a reason. This is to your benefit and allows you to glide through life without holding resentment or grudges.

You are open to other realms, but it is unclear if this has commenced for you or if this is going to happen for you in your future.

You are in touch with your inner child and this is one of the reasons why you present as youthful. Our inner child is very happy to commune with our Soul and our inner child and our Soul work together with great ease and they enjoy fun and spontaneity together. You like and enjoy fun and spontaneity.

You are unpretentious. You present yourself to the world in an authentic manner. You present yourself as how you are and you do not hide yourself with masks as you feel no need to. You feel at home in yourself and show yourself to the world. Again, this is very much to your credit.

It seems that your most developed sense is your ability to work with your sense of hearing and you are able to decipher audible qualities, which other people are unable to.

You are open, friendly and a good friend to others. You are uncomplicated. It is easy to visualise you clapping along to the beat of this song with friends. This song allows you to tap into your inner child, your happiness and your sense of faith and trust in benevolence. This is a wonderful quality to bring to the world.

You like the sound of this music and you like the sound of the gospel and the sound of Madonna's voice. You enjoy these sounds and they uplift you and make you feel happy.

Your Guardian Angel is with you.

CHAPTER TWENTY-SEVEN

"Losing My Religion" performed by R.E.M

If this is your favorite song, then you are probably special in these ways:

- Passionate
- Fascinating
- Complex
- Access the bigger picture of life
- Desire to be with Spirit
- Desire transformation
- A seeker of truth
- Sensitive to the psychic field
- A deep, pensive Soul
- Open to the ambiguous
- Mysterious
- Intense
- Sincere
- Imaginative

Client: Luke

It has been an absolute joy to intuit this Song Read for you.

I interpret your deeper connection to the song in this way:

You are a passionate individual and you feel deeply. This song connects you with Source very quickly. You are a fascinating person, full of complexities.

This song conjures opposite emotions in you. There is pain—a lot of it. There is expanded vision and your ability to access the bigger picture of life. There is a feeling of some oppression and beneath this there is openness and almost a desire to be with Spirit—a desire for transformation. You are a complex character. You are filled with contradictions and dichotomies, but not in a difficult or bad way. These contradictions exist and you are aware that love and hate exist together; they are different ends of the same pole. Opposites happen and exist together.

This song affects you deeply. Both the music and lyrics affect you deeply. You will probably possess a quest in this life, and you have perhaps commenced this quest to understand the deeper meanings of life. You are a seeker of truth.

You possibly find that what happens in life is unexpected. You may be surprised with things which happen in life. You find it difficult to realize that people act in the way that they do. Your inner core being is pure. You are extremely sensitive to the psychic field and so you are perceptive to hurts being inflicted upon others. It is to your benefit to acknowledge what is happening to others and then to cut from this energy and to choose not to take it personally into your own energy field.

Your crown chakra is activated with this song. The crown chakra is the doorway to Spirit. There are energetic tears in the eyes. You may or may not be aware of your Soul presence, but you are very connected with your Soul presence. If you want ease, meditation is perhaps the key to offer you ease and peace.

You are a deep, pensive Soul, who is open to exploring different avenues, paths and viewpoints. You are thoughtful and ponder the alternatives in life. You are extremely sensitive and easily pick up the energies and thoughts of people and situations around you. Your depth of feeling is a double edged sword. On the one hand, it opens you to pain and on the other hand your deep feelings open you to love.

You are open to the ambiguous and you have a mysterious quality.

The musical instrumental component of this song connects you to your Soul. For you, I sense 'God's tempo.' The lyrics of this song connect you to the thoughts in your head and to some degree to your feelings in your heart as well. The music is your Soul talking to you. If you choose to become aware of your energy field, this expanded consciousness which you are feeling through this music is your Soul energy surrounding and within your physical body. This is how close your Soul is. It is within and beside you. Perhaps it is time to pay closer attention. Your Soul desires to talk and commune with you. And my advice is to trust this and not to be fearful.

It is possible that in your earlier life, you have been on the receiving end of negative words.

It is highly likely that spiritual aspects of life will suit you.

You have a powerful intensity within you and you are incredibly sincere. Your imagination is alive and kicking. When I am intuiting this Song Read for you, I feel as if I am looking in the mirror.

You probably do not like the feeling of being on view to others because you remember hurt (maybe from past lives,) which has occurred because of this exposure. However, with some work, this can easily be transformed so that you are able to stand in your own power of precisely who you are, which is a beautiful person, and share this with the world.

Client Feedback

"Hi Awen,

Your interpretation is very accurate. I was 12 when I first heard this song, the year it was released in 1991. I've always thought the phrase "losing my religion" to not be about religion but a loss of faith that leads to a loss of hope. The angst of the character in the lyrics. To hear a song that sounded very different to what you'd hear back then grabbed my attention. The open expression of raw emotion the song has, particularly Michael Stipe's lyrics and voice and the tones of the mandolin."

-Luke

CHAPTER TWENTY-EIGHT

"Love Bites" performed by Def Leppard

If this is your favorite song, then you are probably special in these ways:

- Reverent
- Intuitive
- Potential for clairaudience
- At home with your feelings
- Desire love
- Have a good sense of humor
- Desire to share love, express love and be immersed in love
- Express tears of joy

Client: Hilary

I have thoroughly enjoyed intuiting this Song Read for you. I had not heard this song before.

I interpret your deeper connection to this song in this way:

Before we start with this Song Read, your guides are coming through with much loving energy and presence… this is for you. There is a sense of reverence in the air. You are reverent.

Your temple chakras are activated. You are open to intuition. Possibly you are not aware of the natural development you have in this sphere.

There are also a lot of laughs. You pick up and sense many energy impressions from people and from your surroundings. It is useful for you to tune into this. Especially in the surrounds of nature and around plants. You have the capacity to hear much, especially sounds other people are not able to hear.

You are connected to Source with this song. You are at home with your feelings and with love. You desire love very much in life. You wish for a love with great passion and with an essence of full sensory love.

The guitar is lovely for you and the guitar comes through and energetically sits in your heart chakra. Your heart chakra is open and the sound of this guitar helps to open your heart more and creates a bigger 'cup' for receiving love.

You have a good sense of humor and I am laughing while intuiting this Song Read.

Consider tuning into your imagination, as you will enjoy this.

You like this song because it creates a sense of fullness for you. This fullness you are feeling is a fullness of clean, clear energy. This fullness you are feeling is actually weightless. It is a different fullness to eating a big meal and feeling full and weighted. Being full with clear, clean, life force energy is weightless and it is like a balloon and draws you upwards.

You are very connected to The Divine and the image I have of you is with your hands in the prayer mudra, held straight above your head leading you upwards to The Divine.

You desire to share love, express love and be in and immersed in love. You are looking for this love through a romantic love, which is one way to search for this. Remember, there are other ways too. If you tune into the energy of your friends you will find that a lot of these qualities of love are happening in your friendships. There is also Divine love which is available for you as well. This desire for love is available to you and is a worthy goal.

You express tears of joy.

The guitar sound also plays energetically outside of your ear space and your faculties and potential for clairaudience will perform in a similar way to guitar strings. You will be able to pluck the next high vibrational sound and hop to the next high vibrational sound. These sounds are not often discernible to the average ear.

My hunch for you is that this love which you crave is Soul Love.

You thoroughly enjoy this music and these sounds and it helps you to express love.

Wonderful.

CHAPTER TWENTY-NINE

"Marry You" performed by Bruno Mars

If this is your favorite song, then you are probably special in these ways:

- You Like Christmas!
- Upbeat
- Hopeful
- Have faith
- A happy Soul
- Positive
- Enjoy socializing with your family and friends
- Optimistic
- Affectionate
- Have an easy smile

Client: Ashleigh

Thank you for the opportunity to intuit this Song Read for you. I had not heard this music before.

I interpret your deeper connection to this song in this way:

You like Christmas! You have an upbeat and open personality. You are hopeful and you have faith in benevolence. This song connects you to Source.

You are happy and positive. You also like to have a beneficial effect on others.

It is possible that sometimes you speak from your emotional vantage point, without thinking through beforehand, the effect your words may have on somebody. All of us can at times talk in this way. Whenever we do this, and unintentionally cause hurt, it is useful and helpful to apologize as this clears the energy and it clears the air. We all make mistakes in this way when we verbalize our emotions and inadvertently say unkind words. The reason this seems to be important for you is because you enjoy socializing with your family and friends. So it is important for you to honour your love and enjoyment of other people by being true to them when you may occasionally say hurtful words. This is a good lesson for all of us to learn. When you do this and take responsibility for the less kind words you sometimes say, you become a beacon of light. You become an example for others to follow. Within yourself you become a light channel. There is a higher meaning why this message is coming through for you, as it will elevate your light quotient. You will also teach others with your example.

You are optimistic and you show your affection for your friends easily. You have an easy smile and you are a happy Soul. You bring a lot of light through as well. On the whole you have an easy going personality, but you are not a pushover either.

The sound of the bells are a nice sound for you and suit you well. The sound is festive and happy.

Carry on spreading your smile and sharing your smile.

CHAPTER THIRTY

"Miserere Mei, Deus"
Composed by Gregorio Allegri, performed by The Choir of New College, Oxford

If this is your favorite song, then you are probably special in these ways:

- Devoted
- Logical and rational
- Intelligent
- Reverent
- Have an appreciation for the invisible
- Serious
- Think deeply
- Enjoy living at a considered and measured pace

Client: Mike

It has been a pleasure to intuit this Song Read for you. I had not heard this music before.

I interpret your deeper connection to this song in this way:

Devotion. This music brings you to God. Your crown chakra is activated. This music brings you to the peace of your inner being.

It appears that you have had some pain in life and it is possible that this music has and gives you redemption. The redemptive power of the voice.

You tend to think with your logic, with rationalism and with intelligence. This creates reason and meaning for you. However, this music helps you open to your emotions and perhaps the acknowledgement that you have felt hurt.

There is some heavy energy, which signifies burdens, the emotion of burden and the carrying of burden for perhaps too long a time. Maybe you are ready to let go of this burden now. By acknowledging the burden, it floats up and becomes lighter.

You have the energetic capacity to hear these singing voices through the back of your head. This indicates a particularly reverent spot on your energy body and is also where your devotion emanates from. (Chakras on the back of the head are doorways to higher awareness.)

Energetically, you 'unpeel' with this music. Starting at the top of your head with the crown chakra opening, then the back of your head, moving down through your face to your shoulders, and now we are at your heart chakra opening. So, there is an unpeeling. A slow opening, energetically, to you allowing the music in. Probably, you reflect this in your physical life, where you are more guarded at the beginning of a situation or meeting somebody and then you allow yourself to open when you have and sense trust. It may take a little longer for you to open and warm to people. We are now down to the navel chakra, which is open, and the tummy is warm and the abdomen is warm and feeling nurtured. And now we have arrived at the base chakra and your energy body is fully open to Source through your antakarana (which is the core of our energy anatomy.)

This is a beautiful choice of music.

When the solitary voice in the choir raises above all the other voices it sounds like a white dove.

It is difficult for you to describe the effect these voices have on you. These voices let you know that your reverence and your sense of appreciation, in this case of the invisible, is alive and kicking.

You are a serious person who thinks deeply about topics which are of interest to you. Your mind is penetrating when the subject matter interests you. You are able to think deep, long and far and you can uncover information from beneath obstacles. Your mind is well versed and helpful for you.

You tend to work at a measured pace. You enjoy living at a considered, measured pace.

There is an image of a choirboy, which is not too radical for this choice of music. Were you in a choir as a young boy?

I'm sure that you have translated these lyrics so that you understand this piece of music and the intentions of the lyrics.

I'm receiving the sense of some loss for you which still feels sad.

You concentrate a lot when you listen to this music. By concentrating so much, be aware, that your will may take you down an avenue which you are choosing to go down. You can also choose to concentrate and ruminate less and allow the music and sounds to wash over you which will take you down a different path and show you a new experience. In other words, with less concentration the experience of this music will be more intuitive and perhaps provide you with a new vision or a new emotion.

This is a wonderful piece of music and the sound of the beautiful high voice is sublime. It is a piece of music where it would be beneficial to read the psalm to discover what these words mean and the intent of these words.

There is an image, which has presented itself, of a large solitary deep evergreen tree. Above this is a concrete rendered wall with a narrow opening for a post box. This slim narrow opening looks out onto the wide expanse of blue sky. This is perhaps symbolizing glimpses.

This music can provide for you glimpses into light, essence, harmony, peace and sacredness of The Divine.

CHAPTER THIRTY-ONE

"Moments of Pleasure" performed by Kate Bush

If this is your favorite song, then you are probably special in these ways:

- Romantic
- Possess warmth
- Give love, receive love, express love
- Possess a wonderful sense of heart
- Express tears of joy
- Forgiving
- Compassionate
- A gentle soul
- Open to magic
- Open to your feelings
- Subtly artistic and expressive

Client: Sam

I have thoroughly enjoyed intuiting this Song Read for you. I had not heard this song before.

I interpret your deeper connection to this song in this way:

You are a romantic soul! Your heart is open and warm. There is a great deal of warmth in you. 'Warmth' expresses you exceedingly well. You possess the gifts of the heart chakra.

Your heart is beautifully connected to Source. You give love, receive love, express love and touch others with your love through the embrace of your arms. You are centred in the power of this love.

For you, love is an all-encompassing 'orchestra' and your arms possess the essence of warmth emanating from your heart. This essence runs all the way down your arms to your finger-tips. You have a wonderful sense of heart and love.

The heart chakra is precisely replicated in the centre of the crown chakra and so the benefits of your beautiful heart chakra will also benefit your crown chakra and its connection to Source.

You possess a wonderful, open, free energy field. You are connected to Source. Maybe you disguise your good actions. Or, perhaps you are a modest personality. You express tears of joy.

You are connected right down throughout your body. You have warmth going throughout your whole body and into your legs. One of your missions in life is to walk this earth and to spread this sense of love; by demonstrating this love, by giving and receiving love, forgiving easily, embodying compassion and expressing the qualities of the heart. In this way, you teach others and others emulate you when they see how effortlessly you glide through life embracing the gifts of your heart chakra.

Your heart chakra is in many ways a 'ballerina.' This is a nice metaphor for you.

This song and music sits most wonderfully and completely in your energy field. It is beautiful to see.

Glide softly throughout life and you will touch many people. Perhaps you will not be aware of this effect on others.

The harp is a nice instrument for you. The sound of the harp strings.

You are a gentle soul. You are open to magic. Sprinkle this behind you as you journey throughout life.

In Spirit world there is no time. Time doesn't exist. This is a limitation down here on planet earth. Maybe you are sometimes aware of this.

You are open to your feelings and you enjoy the abstraction and artistry of these lyrics. You are subtly artistic and expressive and open to nuance and subtleties. You fully realise that often words don't easily express our emotions. Maybe we do need another language for emotions and love.

Sweet. Blessings.

CHAPTER THIRTY-TWO

"Nellie the Elephant" performed by Toy Dolls

If this is your favorite song, then you are probably special in these ways:

- Grateful
- Like to have fun
- Like to laugh
- Fun
- Enjoy being with a group
- Easily accept different personalities
- Aim for everyone in the group to enjoy the moment
- Poetic
- Enjoy freedom
- Enjoy the absurd
- Open to different ways, paths and viewpoints
- A storyteller
- Have the ability to perceive the finer details around you
- You desire fables and fairy tales to become true
- Appreciative

Client: Faith

It has been a pleasure to intuit this Song Read for you.

I interpret the hidden messages in your favorite song and music in this way:

You are now at a stage in your life where you offer gratitude before you receive. This is to your benefit.

You like to have fun, you like to laugh and you are a fun personality too. You really enjoy being with a group, sharing fun with people you like.

This song connects you easily to Source. The sound "000000000" before the chorus, creates an upward connection with Spirit for you.

For you, this song deeply represents a joining together of Spirit, fun and being in a group setting and accepting different personalities. You are not distracted by people's foibles and idiosyncrasies. Your aim is for everyone in the group to enjoy the moment.

You enjoy laughing.

The secret message, for you, is in the lyrics. You enjoy and appreciate the poetry of these lyrics; you enjoy the potential for freedom within these lyrics. You enjoy the absurd in these lyrics and you are open to different ways, paths and viewpoints. These qualities are in you too. Poetry, freedom, absurdity and openness to alternative methods are important aspects in your life. You desire to experience these qualities. These are qualities you search for in life. Your energy body is full of emotion while this is coming through. These are very important aspects for you to have in your life and necessary for fulfilment.

At times, you may have some difficulty expressing your emotions.

There is also a storyteller in you, which is another reason why you enjoy these lyrics.

Interestingly, if we draw the "000000000," it can easily look like the sign of infinity stretching on for ever.

You appreciate how this singer thoroughly enunciates every word in the lyrics. This shows your sensitivity to detail and your ability to pick up and perceive the finer details around you.

There is great fun here for you! This song allows your inner child and your mother archetypes to shine and your desire for fables and fairy tales to become true.

There is a gentle fun in you. There is a lot of fun, but you express it in a soft way, rather than a loud and noisy way.

Your energy field is nice and clear and it is coming through that amber is a color for you. There is also an apple green color appearing for you.

You practise appreciation and gratitude.

CHAPTER THIRTY-THREE

"Nights in White Satin" performed by The Moody Blues

If this is your favorite song, then you are probably special in these ways:

- A deep personality
- Purposeful
- Sincere
- Believe in fate
- Earnest
- Have the capacity to be Soul centered
- Experience internal joy
- Quiet
- Great joy waits for you
- Beauty is important to you

Client: Pete

I have thoroughly enjoyed intuiting this Song Read for you.

I interpret your deeper connection to this song in this way:

You are deep, purposeful and sincere. You believe in fate. There is a sense of a procession into destiny in this sound for you.

You are earnest and you have the capacity to be Soul centered and to be with your Soul. You can also hold onto and experience great internal joy.

You have a quiet personality.

'Purpose' is important to you. And so my question to you is, 'What is your purpose?" This is key for you. What is your reason and which part do you wish to play on the stage of life?

The secret message for you is twofold—'purpose' and 'Soul.' You also know the answer to this. The message is purely to let you know how important these two experiences are for you.

You love the words in the chorus and this is where the Soul centering comes in for you.

You are connected to Source and your Soul is talking to you in this song. The message is also present in the lyrics. The lyrics provide you with guidance.

This yearning and serious pull, which you cannot escape, is your Soul talking to you. It is possible, and it may be time, for you to surrender further to your Soul life.

The path hasn't always been easy for you. There has been pain and obstacles, but overwhelmingly you are ready to take the next step and great joy waits for you.

Beauty is also important to you. Beauty is a virtue of our Soul. Beauty allows us to appreciate the gifts in others. Beauty allows us to be in wonder at the world. It may be helpful to research the qualities of beauty.

The sound of the violin strings connects you to Source.

CHAPTER THIRTY-FOUR

"Nothingness" performed by Living Colour

If this is your favorite song, then you are probably special in these ways:

- Intriguing
- Groovy
- Curious
- Unusual
- Have a sense of love within you
- You desire to access inner peace
- Sincere
- Devoted
- Reverent
- Respectful
- Have a strong sense of touch
- Expressive hands
- Brave and courageous

Client: Tyler

It has been a treat to intuit this Song Read for you. I had not heard this music before.

I interpret the hidden messages in your favorite song and music in this way:

You are intriguing, groovy and curious. You are unusual.

There is some sadness in you. You are connected to Source with this song.

It is possible that you can get carried away with your thought processes. Perhaps you are not aware that within, you have the power to halt your thoughts if they are not helping you and you have the power to change the direction of your thoughts. We are all similar in this way. Many of us forget to take care with our thoughts, or are not aware to take responsibility for where we allow our thoughts to go.

You are an unusual individual and I clairvoyantly see you smiling in agreement! It is difficult to select the words to describe you because of your unusualness. So, we will work with imagery.

Within you there is a beam of steadiness and it is similar to a stream. It flows through life and it is steady. Along the way the bird sounds indicate the astral sphere, where thoughts are coming in and you are becoming diverted along little arteries dealing with areas of interest and areas of concern in life.

You have a sense of love within you. An innocence and an inner sense of love. It is possible the sadness in you is because you desire to access this love. You desire to access this inner peace.

You are sincere and there is a hidden aspect of devotion in you, just on the edge of your consciousness. You have within you a sense of reverence and respect. Again these aspects are far out in your consciousness. I sense that it is Spirit that you are trying to contact. Perhaps you do not yet realise that you have the power within you to be intentional in the choices you make and with some of the diversions you select. You have a choice to let some of the distractions subside and you can choose to focus on your inner goals. Consider the visual of the stream in nature. It will, by its own being, merge into a bigger water source. It will go to where its home is. The power is also within you to go to your bigger source of Soul. With the understanding and acknowledgement of this you can proceed with experimenting and making some active choices for yourself which will help you along this path.

You are very connected to Source with this music. There is a lot of energy in your hands which indicate that your sense of touch is strong and you are also expressive with your hands.

You have been brave and courageous sending your favorite song in. I sense with you we are talking about hidden aspects within you and deeper longings within your being.

Your Soul is alive and well, happy and pleased that you are pushing through.

Your chakras and energy field are open. When I am sensing your energy, clairvoyantly it moves from a clear and cooler energy to a crisp, autumn's morning energy and proceeds to a warmer and comforting energy. So you are expressing the different dimensions of you. The different pulls and tugs you experience in life. This is why you are unusual; you are open to different sources, different modes.

Returning to the visual of the stream. A stream is the element of water and water represents our emotions. So you may find the secret for you to progress internally, in a direction which may be helpful for you, is to pay attention and follow your feelings. Become aware when your feelings are joyous, enthusiastic, appreciative, loving and follow these feelings they will help guide you to where you want to be.

Namaste and Blessings.

CHAPTER THIRTY-FIVE

"Nutshell" performed by Alice in Chains

If this is your favorite song, then you are probably special in these ways:

- Desire to express love, share love and to give love
- Desire to hold the world in your arms
- Easily express emotions and feelings
- Creative
- Feel deeply
- Sympathetic
- Empathetic
- Compassionate

Client: Gita

I have thoroughly enjoyed intuiting this Song Read for you. I had not heard this song before.

I interpret your deeper connection to this song in this way:

The guitar music at the beginning of the song energetically enters your heart and your upper arms. You want to hold and to encompass the world in your arms and your embrace. You desire to express love, share love and to give love freely. The guitar sound is wonderful for you. You are very connected to Source. This quality of love sits beautifully in your energy field.

You are able to easily express your emotions and your feelings. You are talented in this area. You tend to operate from how you feel rather than how you think. Your creative and emotional side is the stronger side for you. Possibly you may suffer from some headaches with your intellectual and rational side sometimes wanting some more expression.

There appears to be a slight internal struggle within you. This perhaps involves the ideal of your emotions and visions manifesting in the physical world in a different way to how you wish them to manifest. Consider the possibility that no matter how we wish our ideals to manifest they usually manifest perfectly. It is often the case that we do not see the manifestation or understand the expression of the manifestation. If chains tether you maybe seek to understand the chains. Understanding will give you peace.

You feel deeply and are open to your emotions. You have enormous sympathy for others and the striving mass. There is some sadness in you too and it is from your own trials and tribulations that you have learned to readily give love. You give the gifts of empathy, sympathy and compassion to others.

Client Feedback

"Dear Awen,

Wow that sounded much more accurate than I expected. Mostly I feel ok, but often I think, why isn't my life more interesting, like I imagine people on the internet or tv to have? I am not understanding how to manifest a more fulfilling life at all. I am a painter, but I study health science. I'm not too on the ball with study. I would probably be a bit better off if I was better at taking the time to do it. I don't get headaches usually. Often taking codeine.

Thanks" Gita

CHAPTER THIRTY-SIX

"Oh, What a Night" performed by The Four Seasons

If this is your favorite song, then you are probably special in these ways:

- Desire to live life with a spring in your step
- A nice person
- Balanced in intellect, intuition and emotions
- Content
- Naturally drawn and attracted to helpful and healthful people and situations
- Easily achieve success
- Naturally use your own inner magnetic force of attraction
- Popular
- Prefer deep relationships
- Happy
- Remember the good and expect the good in people and events
- A great mother (nurturing parent)
- Access your own inner sense of fun

Client: Natalie
It has been a pleasure to intuit this Song Read for you.

I interpret the hidden messages in your favorite song and music in this way:

You like the sound of the cymbals, drums and the piano. You like the 'groove' in the sound. You find it easy to move to this music. You move your head as if in agreement and with an understanding of the beat.

You are very connected to Source with this song. You are drawn to the beat. The beat, the flow, the spark, the agility of step is how you want to live life. You desire to live life with a spring in your step. This is the secret message for you.

You are a very nice person! This is not an adjective I use often, 'nice.' I sense you moving to this music. You are balanced in intellect, intuition and in your emotions. You are content, which is a great quality to have.

You are naturally drawn and attracted to helpful and healthful people and situations. Continue to follow your gut instincts as they lead you to positive outcomes. It is to your advantage to be aware and to follow your inner voice.

Success is easy for you to achieve. This comes naturally to you because you are attracting it. You are open to success, but it is your behaviour which attracts success. In this context, we are looking at success across many levels; relationships, love, money etc. success is available to you. It's good for you to naturally use your own inner magnetic force of attraction.

Your balanced personality is very beautiful.

People like you. You perhaps choose to have a small circle of friends, but you could easily have a big circle of friends. But I don't think this is what you want. You are popular but you don't desire to know everybody and seem to prefer deeper relationships.

I can most easily sense you through movement, a gentle, side to side movement of happiness and contentment.

You tend to remember the good and you tend to expect the good. This is also to your credit.

If you are not a mother yet, you will be a great mother. This is because you have access to your own inner sense of fun and your own inner child, and you will be balanced with the responsibility, the fun and the teaching faculties which are helpful for parenthood.

Client Feedback

"Hi

Natalie here. Just read my reading on my song. Scary. ha but so true. I am already a mother to five kids (28 -14) and it's so true I have a fantastic relationship with them all, we are sooo close and I see and hear of them every day. I am always there when they need me and I know when to leave them to it. Also, it was correct about friends, I get on great with a lot of people but I prefer only to keep a few close to me. These are friends I've known for over 20 years and they have never let me down. I was impressed how close you read me from just a song but it certainly made me smile. Great luck with this project it sounds great."

-Natalie x

CHAPTER THIRTY-SEVEN

"One" performed by Metallica

If this is your favorite song, then you are probably special in these ways:

- Have a 'bird's eye view' of life
- At home expressing all of yourself, both the light and the dark
- Have a good sense of humor
- Have a refined spirit
- Fun
- Comfortable in yourself
- Have expanded vision
- Interesting
- Complex
- Express yourself well
- Intelligent
- Desire to feel passion
- Possess a sense of drama

Client: Matthew

I have thoroughly enjoyed intuiting this Song Read for you. I had not heard this song before.

I interpret your deeper connection to the song in this way:

Your energy field is presenting as manly and masculine.

Distant places, far reach. This is an absolutely beautiful sound for you. You are very connected to Source. The rifts of the guitar at the beginning of song are absolutely beautiful with you and beautiful within your energy field. It is as if you can fly. Your energy field is becoming wider, bigger and stronger under this sound of the guitar. Clairvoyantly, there are images of flying wings. This sound can transport you very easily.

Your energy field is expansive and you have a 'bird's eye view' of life. You have great joy expressing the darker side of yourself! You smile when you do this. You are at home expressing all of yourself, both the light and the dark.

You have a good sense of humor. You have a strong laugh. You are making me laugh. Your laugh encompasses the whole group whom you are with. At times you may have difficulties expressing your emotions.

You have a refined spirit and you are great fun and you are also at home in your own shadow aspects as well. This is quite unusual as many of us tend to run from our shadow. And you are still making me laugh.

All of the music sounds are fine in your energy field and they do not disturb your energy field. Some of the sounds are heavier and some of the sounds are lighter. You are comfortable with the sounds. You are comfortable in yourself as well.

There is another image and this is emanating from your central spine, up through your crown chakra. It is a 'lighthouse.' You have expanded vision and take in what others may miss. And it is with your expanded vision that you see distant places and have far reach. You love the lyrics. With the 'lighthouse' you see war and fighting. You don't necessarily agree with this but you are aware of fighting and war. This could also be the war within yourself. Trying to fight the chaos and war within you.

The sounds are interesting and complex. You are showing your complexities to the world. At times there can be some chaos within you. A mad, racing, running, darting around. When this racing happens what you really seem to be searching for is the upward spiral staircase, to take you out from the depths and up to the light.

You are an interesting and complex character. You express yourself well and inclusively. You express from your heart, your intuitions, and intellect. Your emotions are expressed to a slightly lesser extent. You have a beautiful depth to you. It may serve you to become conscious of the words you use because you are able to summon considerable energy through your words. Your energy field is connected to Source with this song and one of the secrets for you to arrive at a sense of peace is silence. Breathe, delve deep inside yourself and experience this silence.

The sounds of the guitar sit so beautifully in your energy field. This expresses all of your lightness and all of your light, your subtleties and intricacies and sensitivities and your love.

You are intelligent and you intelligence enjoys the lyrics. You desire to feel passion and you desire to feel some extremities as there is a sense of drama within you.

The energy in your upper left arm is heavy and it feels as if you have received a physical pummeling at some stage, or in a past life.

You are probably a sweeter person than you desire to be!

Client Feedback

"Hi Awen,

Thanks so much for doing that. It is very interesting reading. Some which is pretty close to the mark and some which I don't personally see about myself but maybe true. If I was to recommend you to people, do you have a site or email they could contact you on or how to go about it.

Cheers"

Matthew

CHAPTER THIRTY-EIGHT

"One Tree Hill" performed by U2

If this is your favorite song, then you are probably special in these ways:

- Understand that life is bigger than it seems
- Powerful
- Strong
- Sincere
- Capable of great love and passion
- Resilient
- Desire freedom
- Connected with your gut feeling and your gut emotions
- Feel deeply
- Love deeply
- Tolerant
- Have tears of joy and tears of pain
- Desire to hold love and share love
- When you love you also impart strength
- Steadfast

Client: Louisa

It has been a pleasure to intuit this Song Read for you. I had not heard this music before.

I interpret your deeper connection to the song in this way:

You like the sound of the percussion because it illustrates that there is more going on running beneath the surface. Percussion brings you to this reality.

You also love Bono's voice—its power, strength and sincerity. You possess these qualities too. You feel great love with the voice of Bono and passion. When Bono sings with depth and passion, your heart wells with love and you feel connected, you feel whole, you feel on purpose and you feel on track.

Your Soul is very much with you when you listen to this song, which connects you very beautifully to Source. This is the main reason you are attracted to this song. You go to this song because of this Soul connection. This song connects you to love, freedom and the essence of your higher, bigger, fuller self. Our Soul self can be free, but our physical selves find it far more difficult to be free.

It seems that life has not always been easy for you. You may have endured quite a few challenges and tests. You have come through these with flying colors. You have great resilience within you, and perhaps more than you are aware of. If you stay in your energy field and possess your energy and avoid being too mixed up in the opinions of others, you will skip quite happily through life.

For you, a sense of your freedom happens when you stay contained within your energy field. The guitar riffs illustrate your desire for freedom and the purity of freedom.

You are also a 'Cloud" girl. Get up on the clouds; stand on the clouds, because you are able to. Lightness and freedom are here. Magic awakes. Hold hands with your favorite people when you are up here. To illustrate this, think of the childhood rhyme "Ring of Roses," hopping and skipping, holding hands, going around in a circle and the potential of imagination. This is beautiful for you.

You have a good connection with your gut feeling and your gut emotions. So it is beneficial to pay attention to these.

If you allow the time to be with this connection with your higher self and the time for these feelings of freedom and also of being in the outdoors and running and being physically in nature you will feel more in harmony. If you allow this spiritual and physical element to happen in your life it will create balance for you and ultimate joy.

An interesting choice for you is the symbol of 'the sunshine.'

I will describe a vision of an environment especially suited to you: It is similar to an Irish coastline; a colder environment, wrapped up, feeling cozy, helping to keep others warm and others helping you to keep warm, this is a very loving embrace for you. Scarves and sweaters, the beach and rocky cliffs, hard and darker colored sand. This style of environment is a helpful and natural environment for you to be in. When you are next on a beach and you are walking around a cliff edge of rocks, perceive and imagine a white horse or a white unicorn waiting to meet you around the corner. They are actually there and are seen through the ajna chakra, rather than through the physical eyes. Your unicorn is at this juncture of ocean and beach, around the corner and is waiting for you. Unicorns are very highly evolved spiritual beings. Your job is perhaps to trust that this unicorn is there rather than expecting to run into him, though this is always possible. Your unicorn is female.

You feel very deeply and you love deeply and you desire to connect with tolerance amongst people. Tolerance is a high virtue for you and you are tolerant too. You can easily shed tears of joy and tears of pain.

This song energetically plays in your heart chakra and your upper arms, which are connected to your heart chakra. You have a desire to hold love and share love through your arms. You desire to hold people and to be held. When you love, you also impart strength.

Your emotional side can at times become too involved and this is not in a healthful way for you. If you feel too emotionally connected, perhaps caught up with words, consider to cut back and go into your body and into your sense of who you are and allow your intelligence and rationalism to catch up.

A message for you is to stay steadfast and you will know what this means. You don't need to become steadfast; you are this way, so stay this way.

You are an emotional individual and you are connected emotionally through your Soul. You are nicely connected to Source.

You are well looked over in life. Your higher guides walk with you. They walk behind you, they walk beside you and they walk in front of you.

I can see why you like this song. It's beautiful. Run and be free.

CHAPTER THIRTY-NINE

"Safe and Sound" performed by Taylor Swift

If this is your favorite song, then you are probably special in these ways:

- Ethereal
- Possess strong intuitive faculties
- Open to fairies
- Open to guidance
- Open to receiving help
- At home in nature
- Aspire to a quality of purity and like pure clarity
- Considerate
- Gentle
- Peace loving
- Sensitive
- Possess internal harmony
- Have a beneficial, calming and serene effect on others

Client: Meagan

It has been a pleasure to intuit this Song Read for you. I had not heard this music before.

I interpret your deeper connection to this song in this way:

Wonderful and ethereal. The music and you are ethereal. You have strong intuitions and are open to fairies and the elemental fairies (earth fairies in nature.) You are open to guidance and open to receiving help. This music connects you to Source. If you ever need any help, the secret is to ask and you will receive the help intuitively.

You are at home in nature. You perhaps have a fairy look to you. You aspire to a quality of purity and you like pure clarity. You may be shy in your personality.

You appreciate when your friends and family put their best foot forward and you also appreciate when people are considerate during conversation. You choose to be considerate. You admire consideration in speech and communication so that harmony occurs in a group. Harmony is an important facet for you. You possesses internal harmony and you need to have this in your external life.

There are clairvoyant images of Mother Earth, fairies and white bands that elves sometimes wear around their forehead. This white band image is strong.

The sound of the guitar strings suit you. You are gentle, peace loving and sensitive. You are also sure of certain attitudes and behaviours to adopt.

You are connected to Source. It is a good idea to make sure you are grounded to the earth. Green grass and green fields are particularly suitable for you and a wonderful environment for you. The energy running through your body is strong and you provide (spiritually) a lot of light and maybe you are not aware of this. You have a beneficial, calming and serene effect on others, particularly when you are in a group of about three people. When you are in a small group you do not even need to talk because of the energetic effect which is happening through you.

The image which is the strongest is the white band running around the forehead which suggests that your intuitive faculties and appreciation and openness to other realms is exceedingly strong. The shape of this band is a circle, representing perhaps a ring or a symbolic marriage to wholeness and conclusion.

The circle is a wonderful shape for you. It can symbolize the way life revolves and carries on. Everlasting.

CHAPTER FORTY

"Save Tonight" performed by Eagle Eye Cherry

If this is your favorite song, then you are probably special in these ways:

- Sincere
- Loyal
- Upbeat
- Honest
- Optimistic
- A happy soul
- Well grounded
- Giving
- A good friend
- Comfortable in relationship
- Secure
- Steady and sure
- Have direction
- Successful
- A good leader
- Exist in the present day

Client: Janie

I have thoroughly enjoyed intuiting this Song Read for you. I interpret your deeper connection to this song in this way:

You are sincere, loyal, upbeat, honest and optimistic. This song connects you with Source. You are a happy soul who is well grounded on planet earth.

You enjoy being with your friends. You have a big energy field and you share this easily. You give easily to others too. You are a good friend. You also do not tend to harbor grudges.

You know how to work and be comfortable in a one on one relationship. You are probably happy in a small group of two to six people.

You have a nice balanced energy field. You are secure, both on the earth and within yourself. You are steady and sure and move easily through life. You have a clear direction in where you want to go in life. You are able to pull all of your energies and resources together and you naturally understand how to use these to arrive at your destination in life. You are successful because you naturally use your talents in a beneficial way.

You possess good, solid, thinking which allows you to not stray too much from the matter at hand. Usually your goals are fair and appropriate for all parties concerned.

In many ways, this aspect of easily being able to use your natural talents, resources and abilities shows that you are a good leader. You can easily lead a team. You may also be talented with physical exercise. You perhaps have the ability to lead people to become fit and healthy.

You exist in the present day, not the past or the future. Another words, you spend your time and energy in the present day, which is to your benefit.

Your headspace is the slightly stronger faculty and the only caution is that it may not be to your benefit to overthink, over intellectualise or over rationalise matters. Your emotional side and intuitive sides are also strong so allow these to stay balanced in your being.

You present as very stable and connected, both to The Divine and to the earth. You have good thoughts, good aspirations and good hopes.

'Ease' is nice a word for you.

You may like singing along with these lyrics.

You are perhaps attracted to someone who can express his or her emotions well. You are attracted to somebody who can express love.

CHAPTER FORTY-ONE

"Scarborough Fair" performed by Per-Olov-Kindgren (and Simon and Garfunkel)

"Scarborough Fair" transcribed and performed by Per-Olov-Kindgren *(First read)*

If this is your favorite song, then you are probably special in these ways:

- Creative
- Imaginative
- Reverent
- Forgive readily
- Sincere
- Have deep feelings
- Focused
- Desire intimate love
- Express your mental faculties with ease
- Appreciate vocabulary and words
- Able to perceive other realms
- Express tears of joy

Client: Philip

It has been a treat to intuit this Song Read for you. What a wonderful song and sound!

It seems that we have taken an unusual route to arrive at what has turned out to be three different Reads. Though I sense that we have arrived at where we need to be.

I interpret your deeper connection to the song in this way:

You are very connected to Source. Your creative and imaginative side is stronger than your intellectual side and you may have a tendency to work from your emotions.

Perhaps you have headaches at times.

There are tears of joy here for you with this music. You love the intention, the sublime, the reverence and the forgiveness. These qualities are within you especially the capacity to forgive.

Sometimes your higher vision can become clouded.

Clairvoyantly, I am receiving a visual of your kidneys.

I am only receiving a small Read for you. This may be because we are not working with the performer of your choice.

I sense we are not done, so we will return in the afternoon.

"Scarborough Fair" performed by Per-Olov-Kindgren *(Second read)*

Lament, sincerity, deep feelings. These qualities are within you.

You have the ability to pay singular attention to the task at hand. To have complete focus. This is of great benefit to you and you do not become distracted easily.

You have a desire for intimate love. It is possible though that you may put up a guard to prevent this happening and so there is some sadness in you. We are able to erect energetic walls in our lives, but we also have the ability to bring these down.

It appears you would like to express your emotions more than you do. At times you may find it difficult to express how you feel and this is a burden and sadness for you. Whenever, we open ourselves to expressing our emotions and vulnerabilities we are also opening ourselves to the possibility of heartbreak and pain. But unless we take this chance, we are unable to feel whole love too.

For you, the guitar strings represent as the element of water. The element water represents emotions and feelings. Maybe a little more trust in your loved ones and choosing to be open with expressing your emotions will give you the courage to work with this side of your being a little more fully. This seems to be where you want to express yourself.

I strongly sense that we are still not done. So let's move on with Read three.

"Scarborough Fair" performed by Simon and Garfunkel *(Third read)*

A more flowing and open interpretation. Querying. Now you are open to emotion.

Now the guitar strings are expressing the element of air. The element air represents thoughts and the mental plane. You express your mental faculties with ease. There is a hidden poet in you, or, an appreciation of vocabulary and words.

You are connected to Source with this musical version. This music allows you to be fuller energetically. There is a magical, rousing quality for you which can overtake you.

This energy you are feeling, from all of these instruments and sounds together, seems to be Spirit. So the multitude of instruments and bringing many different viewpoints, various stimuli together creates a sense of wholeness for you which is magical. Your ability to hook into other realms happens with this version.

The wind instruments are something which may be nice for you to discover and investigate.

There is a sense of 'Supreme' for you here. Supreme joy, supreme wholeness and supreme God, or however you want to name God.

Here you express tears of joy. Your energy field is transformed with this version.

Incidentally this is a six minute version of the song, rather than a two minute version from earlier. So this allows you to stay in this space of homage and awe for a longer time, which is also to your benefit.

With this version, your Soul takes over and your Soul expresses with ease through you. This is terrifically beautiful, clairvoyantly seeing and sensing what is happening to your energy field. You feel these senses I am seeing.

Of particular interest, with this Song Read, there have been three attempts. When things happen in threes it is a message that your Soul is speaking to you.

Blessings.

Client Feedback

"Thank you so very much Awen, I agree my soul is talking to me and telling me what it needs. I'll need to be a lot more successful in life (financially) as I completely love nature. In my mind I know exactly what I want and where to live and also what I need from life. Again, burdened by finances. But I know one day I will succeed."

Philip

CHAPTER FORTY-TWO

"Shine On You Crazy Diamond" performed by Pink Floyd

If this is your favorite song, then you are probably special in these ways:
- Sensitive to other realms and dimensions
- Passionate
- Expressive
- Sexy
- Interested in mystery
- Talented
- A sophisticated thinker
- Appreciate abstract thoughts
- Clever
- Have substantial knowledge
- Willing to take risks
- Interested in discovery
- Focus and concentrate well
- Complex
- Have acute perception
- Talented with discerning and processing sound
- Observant

Client: Kim

I have thoroughly enjoyed intuiting this Music for you.

I interpret your deeper connection to this song in this way:

Ethereal. You are interested in and sensitive to other realms and dimensions. This music helps you to experience a sense of majesty and awe. You experience this in your thoughts rather than your emotions.

You are passionate and you are expressive too. You are able to express your passion through movement. You are also sexy.

You desire to experience heightened states but haven't been able to manifest this. Manifesting higher vibrational states usually involves a release of intuitive capabilities and a release of emotions. You are able to do this but you tend to be ruled by your logic and rationalism. Thinking about something and experiencing something are different approaches. You are interested in mystery but you perhaps do not experience this.

You are connected to Source with this song. There is a lot of energy in your crown chakra when you listen to these guitar sounds. The crown chakra is the doorway to Spirit.

You like these lyrics. You enjoy the idiosyncrasy and the talent in these lyrics. You are talented too.

You are a thinker and you like this song intellectually.

You possess a nice quality of thought and you can visualize artistically too.

If you desire to experience the sensations of some of these sounds held within the music, it may involve taking some risks and opening your heart to vulnerability. It is through opening our heart further and exposing more of our inner feelings of weakness that we often become open to experiencing in a fuller, more encompassing way. If you desire this, it may be helpful to become aware of your feelings, to name your feeling, consider how these emotions feel and express this from your heart center. 'More' is the operative word. This will allow your emotional capacity to kick in to a higher level and hence your experience.

Your upper chakras are clear; crown, ajna, temples, back of head and throat. I am wondering if this 'space age' sound of music at the beginning of the song helps you form a style of meditation?

Consider to apply your unusual thought processes and your appreciation for abstract thoughts to the medium of art, as you will achieve excellent work and success. There does seem to be a connection with your thinking style and subsequently visually illustrating these thoughts.

There is cleverness in you. Your knowledge is high. You are an independent thinker and can easily think in an abstract way. You naturally do not tend to think along and in agreement with the mass population, but you are not militant with this. You are a sophisticated thinker.

You have a nice clear crown chakra so your heart chakra will be clear too. Your heart is not closed, you just choose to not process through this side of your personality. You are certainly not hindered with obstructions to love.

There is a willingness to take risks.

Science is another possible path for you, as you are interested in discovery.

You can focus easily and you are able to be still and concentrate.

You experience some of your emotions through intuition.

You are a complex individual.

The saxophone sound energetically plays up high above your crown chakra. The sax music represents your Soul.

You have acute perception. You can discern fine detail in sound, in theory and in debate. Some of your talents spring from this ability.

It may be helpful to become aware of glimpses of arrogance. It is wonderful that you are talented and are able to think in a sophisticated way, but in some areas you are less able. Other people, who can't keep up with how you think may be able to express these sides in a more cohesive manner. It is beneficial for you to acknowledge and praise the different talents you see in others. People will warm to you with this little adjustment.

If you are expressive with dance, you may enjoy dancing to this music as there is much room for artistic interpretation and passion.

You are talented with discerning and processing sound. You have an innate ability to capture individual sounds, which is a marvelous quality.

As we come three quarters of the way through this extended 25-minute mix, you relax. It takes a while for you to relax as you possess a very keen sense of observation and you pick up much intellectually.

CHAPTER FORTY-THREE

"Silent Lucidity" performed by Queensryche

If this is your favorite song, then you are probably special in these ways:

- Open to other realms
- Talented with fine detail
- Feel terrific love for the human mass
- Appreciate unity
- Express from the vantage of your emotions and thoughts
- Possess much love
- Harmony is important for you
- Joyful
- Drawn to the beauty of spirituality

Client: Tanya

It has been a treat to intuit this Song Read for you. I had not heard this music before.

I interpret the hidden messages in your favorite song and music in this way:

The impressions that come to mind are: detail, finer qualities and air. You are open to other realms. Your thought processes often outreach into other spaces to perceive impressions and information. You discern fine detail.

Your heart becomes wide and warm with the fuller sounds. You encompass much in your embrace and you feel terrific love for the mass human population. You are wonderfully connected to Source with this song and you feel a sense of bliss with this music.

The section with the orchestra holds a lot of energy for you. This orchestra can be a wonderful metaphor for the concept of people having and living their differences but still joining together and creating a beautiful sound of unity.

On occasion your emotions can take over and at times you give an emotional response when it is not needed. A calm and considered response is sometimes required rather than an emotional response.

You tend to express as the element of water mixed with the element of air. In astrology the element of water represents our emotions and the element of air represents our thoughts.

This music brings you to a juxtaposition of emotions which culminate with a vision of perfection for you. A vision of perfection which you have for the people of the world.

There is a lot of love in you. You like and appreciate all of the musical instruments in this piece, but it appears the magic is in the orchestra sound; when it comes together. This creates a sense of fullness and completion and this may allude to the potential for us to exist as a group in harmony with each other. This sentiment of harmony between people is important for you.

You have the capacity for joy. This joy is a joy which you tend to express outwardly. But, if you look closely it is also an inner joy. Meditation and esoteric wisdom may be fields you may like to study.

The lyrics are wonderful for you.

You must know the possibility of spiritual overtones with this choice of music and the call and beauty of spirituality seems to be calling you.

Namaste.

CHAPTER FORTY-FOUR

"Sky Blue" performed by Peter Gabriel

If this is your favorite song, then you are probably special in these ways:

- Intuitive
- Open to dream worlds and other realms
- Serious
- Feel deeply
- Level headed
- Desire a sense of freedom
- Desire to see the big picture of life
- Understand the unity of 'one'
- Sensitive
- A healer
- Possess an encompassing and expansive mind

Client: Christine

I have thoroughly enjoyed intuiting this Song Read for you. I had not heard this song before.

I interpret your deeper connection to this song in this way:

Namaste.

There is a dreamlike quality. You are open to intuition and other worlds and possess a serious personality.

There is a strong clairvoyant image and this image is of *a procession* advancing deep into the forest. The piano is beautiful for you. The piano sound appears energetically on your shoulders and you smile now. You have become full. There is an image of you, in the *procession*, wearing a cape and when the music becomes fuller, the cape lifts up and twirls and the space beneath the cape starts to encompass much. This shows your openness to other realms and openness to other people and circumstances.

You feel deeply. Your emotions are alive and kicking and you feel with great depth, sensitivity and clarity. Your emotions are not cloudy or confused. You also know how to leave your emotions to the side when this is necessary. So, you are not ruled by your emotions, which is why you come across as level headed.

You desire a sense of freedom, a sense of space and a sense of expression. And now, returning to the earlier image, we can see that the reason you are moving with the *procession*, into the forest is the desire to rest, with the bird's eye view, of looking out over the trees, and being able to see the big picture of life. This seems to be the direction for you.

There is a sense of snow falling, of angels in chorus, of birds. You love the unity of the voices coming together and singing the harmony and you feel at home with this unity. This is the unity of 'one.' You are very much connected to Source.

You like the sky and you enjoy raising your hands to the sky. There is some magic in the sky for you. It is limitless, expansive and the sky sees much.

You are beautifully sensitive and open to your intuition. You have the ability to be a healer and you easily have the ability to pull Spirit down through your body to help others.

Stillness and pure silence are wonderful and welcoming for you. The image of corn gently swaying in a field with the sun setting on the horizon is a beautiful image for you.

You have a wonderful, encompassing and expansive mind. You enjoy the lyrics greatly and the creativity and expressiveness of the lyrics within this song.

Returning to the *procession,* we can now see that there is a slow, steady, measured pace. I sense that you are moving in the right direction, at your own pace. For you there is a sense of ritual in this sound which suits you and it feels as if these lyrics, this song, this sound, the music, the harmonies connect you lovingly, brilliantly and fully to Source. Your connection with Source is pouring down through your crown chakra right into the pit of your tummy and it is a very wide, strong connection.

CHAPTER FORTY-FIVE

"So Afraid" performed by Fleetwood Mac and Lindsey Buckingham

If this is your favorite song, then you are probably special in these ways:

- Passionate
- Imaginative
- Feel alive when you express your emotions
- Feel strongly
- Desire to have a consuming love in your life
- Serious
- Appreciate ambiguity
- Enjoy the abstract
- Desire to experience profound relationships
- Understand that challenging circumstances hold lessons
- Sincere
- Loyal
- Appreciate honesty

Client: Ruby

Thank you for the opportunity to intuit this Song Read for you. I had not heard this music before.

I interpret your deeper connection to this song in this way:

This song is autobiographical for you. You relate to the lyrics. You enjoy the sounds of the musical instruments and you are connected to Source. The lyrics are the key to the deeper meaning of this song you.

You are passionate and you would like people to understand and appreciate the depth of you.

Your imagination is captured by a musical instrument being played in the background behind the song. The instrument may be a guitar, and it has a 'rising up' quality for you. The incessantness of this sound captivates you. You have a sense of *'procession'* with this music.

You enjoy the passion of the instruments and the sound helps you to express your emotions. You feel alive when you express your emotions, especially the deep emotions. You feel so strongly.

You desire to have a consuming love in your life. Maybe you haven't found this yet but this is an experience you desire.

You have a serious personality and you desire to share and to express the depth of emotion which is within you. You love the sound of the guitar. Your energy field becomes fuller under the sound of the solo guitar. You also like ambiguity. As an example, everyone interprets the sound of the guitar differently and you love this. You enjoy the abstract. There is no clear cut definition of the interpretation of this sound for you. The sound is deep and passionate for you and it travels to the core of your being. There is also a 'longing' element and a 'love' element. The sound transports you to the centre of your heart, to the centre of your emotions and to the centre of your being.

The dance version of this track has an extended guitar session. You show all of your beauty to the world through the sound of this guitar solo. This sound allows you to show an essence of yourself to the world. An integral essence of you.

It is important that you have relationships with people with whom you feel comfortable to express the profound essence of you and to experience profound relationships with. Superficial relationships in life will not suffice for you.

There is a redemptive quality in you. You have an understanding that the less desirable and more challenging circumstances which occur in your life hold a lesson to be learned. You have this understanding.

You are incredibly sincere and loyal and you appreciate people who put their best foot forward. You appreciate honesty. Maybe there are a few issues with tact and diplomacy. At times it may be to your benefit to experiment with lightening up a bit. But you are driven to show your whole self.

This song affects your crown chakra and your heart chakra. This is a wonderful choice of song for you.

It may be to your advantage to have a creative outlet to express music, drama, art, or creative writing—to express this deep inner passion within you. Your creative contributions to the world are valid.

CHAPTER FORTY-SIX

"Southern Sun" performed by Boy and Bear

If this is your favorite song, then you are probably special in these ways:

- A happy Soul
- Orientated to the future
- Likeable
- Upbeat
- Optimistic
- Strong
- Grounded and secure
- Creative
- Attractive
- Have a healthy ego and a good sense of self
- Courageous
- Kind
- Talented with organizing and detail
- A good planner

Client: Stacy

Thank you for the opportunity to intuit this Song Read for you. I had not heard this music before.

I interpret your deeper connection to this song in this way:

You are a happy Soul and this is a happy song for you.

You have dreams and hopes for the future. These can come true if you apply and manifest the necessary power into your thoughts and your actions.

You are orientated to the future. You have aspirations and hopes. There is a gentle, likeable quality in you. So you hold aspirations and hopes for others too.

This music helps you to express *languidity*. You enjoy the beat of this music.

It is possible that you are sometimes not hearing everything which needs to be heard in circumstances and situations. At times you can be closed, in a listening way, to some information coming forward for you.

You tend to dislike arguments. You find these a fuss and prefer to ignore and scoot around arguments. This may be helpful for you, but remembers to ensure you speak your truth if the matter is important to you.

You work hard to stay upbeat and optimistic and you may sometimes find that when you are feeling darker emotions, you may not always be processing these emotion. It may be easier to acknowledge the emotion and to understand that the processing of the emotion can be a very quick process. Feel the emotion and it will move through you.

You like happiness and it is definitely a goal for you. This is not always a conscious goal for all people.

You are strong, stable, grounded, secure, creative, attractive, internally powerful, have a healthy ego and a good sense of self. You are courageous and kind and also talented with organizing and detail.

Sometimes your emotional self and your sense of creativity can push outwards and over run your rational and logical side. In some cases logic and intellect are needed and these facets seem to want some expression from you. You may tend to jump to your faculties of intuition and emotion. You have the capacity to be a balanced personality if you choose to be.

Energetically, this song sits in your head space. You like the lyrics and probably sway along to this music.

Also energetically, you are presenting with your dreams and aspirations and you are able to accomplish these if you become conscious of your thought processes and follow thoughts which are beneficial to you. These dreams are coming from your emotional, heart based, creative side. In order to fulfill these dreams you may need to harness logical, rational, action orientated steps. You have within you the ability to plan. So, to achieve your goals, make plans and harness discipline. Consciously work a little every day, perhaps five minutes a day, on harnessing your own discipline. The reason this is important for you is because you *are* fully able and capable, and have within you the means to achieve your goals.

Client Feedback

Well this is very accurate about my personality. I'm a very happy person and love to be happy and I'm glad you got to listen to this song as I find it to be a very relaxed song.

Stacy

CHAPTER FORTY-SEVEN

"Standing Outside a Broken Phone Booth with Money in my Hand" performed by Primitive Radio Gods

If this is your favorite song, then you are probably special in these ways:

- Gutsy
- Grounded to Mother Earth
- Empathetic
- Sympathetic
- Have a good sense of humor
- Intuitive
- A fortunate individual
- Express tears of joy
- Express as an angel
- A guardian of others
- Have a light touch

Client: Alina

It has been an absolute treat to intuit this Song Read for you. I had not heard this music before.

I interpret the hidden messages in your favorite song and music in this way:

You are gutsy and wonderful! You are very connected to Source. This music sits beautifully in your energy field. Clairvoyantly, there are the colors orange, pink and red in your energy field. You have strong energy in your ankles and feet. You are grounded to Mother Earth. You naturally fall into step and empathise and sympathise with your friends and your fellow human beings.

You also have a good sense of humor.

You are open to intuition and you are perceiving and receiving information from many different sources. You may or may not be aware of this.

You have a wonderful energy field and energy flows through you beautifully. You are a fortunate individual. You merge into the sound and energy of others. There is a flowing element within you. Clairvoyantly there is an image of a kite in the breeze and also a ribbon, similar to the type a gymnast holds when they are performing the floor and dance exercises. I sense this ribbon symbolises the sound of piano keys for you. The ribbon represents as a yellow ribbon moving through dimensions. Your connection to Source is wonderful. The colors in your energy field are changing to yellow. You are expressing tears of joy. I wish you could see this and I hope you are able to feel this energy. It is truly awesome and beautiful. This is you.

In many ways you express as an angel! One of your jobs down here on planet Earth is to be a guardian of others. Again, you may or may not know this. You have the capacity to express as the energy field of a guardian as a Guardian Angel! This is awesome!

I have received a word for you and it is 'Sublime'

The symbolic image I have of you is of the gymnast holding the yellow stream of ribbon and particularly the gymnast gracefully performing long jumps over the black and white piano keys. This is the visual lightness, a light touch. This is the light touch you give to others.

Blessings and Namaste. Namaste and Blessings. Round and round and round we go.

CHAPTER FORTY-EIGHT

"Straight to You" performed by Nick Cave and The Bad Seeds

If this is your favorite song, then you are probably special in these ways:

- A deep personality
- Pensive
- Passionate
- Have a good sense of humor
- Aware of the dark side of life and the light side of life
- Serious
- Open to differing viewpoints
- Intellectual
- Open to abstract thought
- Have faith in ultimate benevolence of Spirit
- Have a belief in magic
- Have healthy self-esteem
- Possess helpful boundaries
- Appreciate yourself and others
- An exciting individual
- Adventurous

Client: Andrea

I have thoroughly enjoyed intuiting this Song Read for you. I had not heard this song before.

I interpret your deeper connection to this song in this way,

You are deep, pensive and passionate. You have a good sense of humor. You are aware of the dark side of life and the light side of life. You are aware of the dichotomy in situations. Some situations may look unpleasant but these may hold and offer gems of experience and discovery.

There is an image of the sound of the musical instruments and guitars, being akin to a stone, rolling and gathering moss. The stone is rolling down hills and passing beside trees. This signifies the journey you are venturing in this life.

Conversely, at the same time, when the music rolls along it also signifies the collective, all of us, encompassing the whole.

You are connected with Source with this song.

You enjoy this music. It lifts you. Your smile extends out into your energy field, past your physical cheeks.

You possess a serious side. At times you may be opinionated, which isn't necessarily a bad thing.

You have a lot of energy in your crown chakra and the top of your head. You enjoy thinking about serious aspects of life. You enjoy considering these topics and giving them attention, entering into discussion and debate. You are also open to other viewpoints. You like to achieve growth in your thought processes. You enjoy coming together and discussing favorite subjects and topics with a group and the subsequent understanding, which comes from this, is enhanced for you and others. Your intellect is strong.

You are also open to abstract thought. You enjoy theatre and good vocabulary.

You have a faith in ultimate benevolence of Spirit.

In addition, you have a belief in magic. Maybe you don't understand how magic happens, but you have a belief and acceptance of magic and the possibility of magic. One of the aspects, which grab you with this song, is a sense of magic. It shows you another possibility and you are open to other possibilities even if you don't understand them. A fascination for you with this song is perhaps this exposure to magic.

You possess a nice clean energy field, especially in the area around your tummy and abdomen. You have good healthy internal self-esteem, self-love, self-respect and self-acceptance. You also possess helpful boundaries and you do not tend to play the victim role, rather you accept responsibility for your own life.

You desire the experience of a deep, overwhelming, consuming love. This is available to you if you are willing to experiment with different behaviours and expressions and responses.

This is a lovely, exciting and adventurous song. And these qualities are also in you.

CHAPTER FORTY-NINE

"The Burning of Rome" performed by Virgin Steele

If this is your favorite song, then you are probably special in these ways:

- Dramatic
- Enjoy life
- Fun
- Like speed
- Open to new, fresh ideas and concepts
- Enthusiastic
- Fast in your mental faculties
- Have clear thought processes
- See the big picture
- Creative
- Like excitement
- Enjoy big gestures and grand scale ideas
- Have the ability to think visually
- Perceive fine detail

Client: Malcolm

Thank you for the opportunity to interpret this song for you. I had not heard this music before.

I interpret your deeper connection to this song in this way:

You are dramatic and there is a lot of drama in you. You enjoy life and you are a lot of fun. You also like speed, as in the quickness of speed. There is a musician element in you. Perhaps you are a guitarist.

You are very connected to Source with this music. You have a deep laugh and you are showing me again that you are a lot of fun and you are making me laugh too.

You are open to new, fresh ideas and concepts.

Speed, enthusiasm, high energy and much fun are qualities in you.

Sometimes you may find it hard to express what is going on in your mind because your mind can work quickly and your diction is probably slower than the speed your mind is working at.

Your mental faculties operate with fast speed and at the same time your thought process is clear and you comprehend well and often interpret situations in a beneficial way. You interpret with an aspect of whole vision. Another words you can see the big picture.

You are talented with your arms. Clairvoyantly, I am receiving the image of a musical conductor. This type of energy is coming through. You are a creative person.

You like excitement. Maybe you relish undertaking a dare as well.

You enjoy these lyrics and you would probably enjoy poetry. This music suits you. You enjoy big gestures; big theatre and grand scale ideas and are at home in this realm.

You have the ability to think visually, and surprisingly when you think in this way you often see in slow motion. It is the opposite of the speed of your mental thoughts. This is very useful, as the ability to see in slow motion allows you to perceive the fine detail.

A visual image which has popped through for you is; a choirboy holding a pamphlet of music with a crease down the centre, wearing red undergarments and white over garments. Does this visual image hold significance for you? There is also the reference to the pure inner child connecting to Source through music.

CHAPTER FIFTY

"The Dead Heart" performed by Midnight Oil

If this is your favorite song, then you are probably special in these ways:

- A happy Soul
- Truthful
- Trustworthy
- Loyal
- Joyful
- Possess helpful virtues
- Deeply desire to understand other realms
- Understand that there is more to life than the material world
- A gentle and peaceful soul
- Aware
- Have potential for clairaudience
- Access higher guidance and higher knowledge

Client: Juan
I have thoroughly enjoyed intuiting this Song Read for you.
I interpret your deeper connection to the song in this way:

You are a happy soul! I sense you jumping around as if you are 'pogo' dancing. Clairvoyantly I see you bobbing up and down. You are now presenting energetically as a straight column. You possess the virtues of truth, trustworthiness and loyalty. You have within you a big heart and much joy. Your heart is strong.

You possess an uplifting array of valuable and helpful virtues. The message for you is to ensure you are continually aligned with these virtues as they serve you well.

The energetic column expressed earlier is directed up to The Divine. This is a pure, clear and strong connection. It is also beneficial for you to follow your inner guidance and the inner virtues within you. This will always work in your favour. This is the hidden message for you.

Sometimes you may have confusion and difficulty comprehending other worlds and other realms. However once this difficulty is acknowledged the congestion disperses. And so, it may be helpful to purposefully acknowledge your feelings and thoughts whenever you feel confused or unsure in situations.

There is some sadness in you. This sadness comes when you have difficulty comprehending other realms, as you deeply want to understand this aspect of life. The message for you is to employ your faith, whatever your faith is with, in these instances. The tears can be sad but there is also joy within the tears.

You are beautifully connected with Source with this music. You are 'pogo' dancing in a straight line, this straight column. You perhaps have an inner desire to rise up. There is within you a deep understanding that there is more to life than this material world we find ourselves in. When you do move out of the material world, you become a gentle, expanded, aware and peaceful soul. You are happy and content when you energetically expand out of the physical realm.

Volume (as in hearing) is very important for you. Sometimes you like loud volume and sometimes you prefer a softer volume, but the correct volume to experience singing or talking etc. is an enjoyable factor for you. This may indicate some potential for clairaudience. Clairaudience is the ability to hear and interpret vibrations and sounds with the inner or outer hearing and to hear what is inaudible. This potential may come to fruition for you in the future.

You have a wide smile.

You appreciate intricacies.

Energetically for you the area most activated with this music is around and outside your temple and ear chakras. There is some sparkling energy and this is where angels talk and whisper to you. You feel a sense of home in this space. This area can access higher guidance and higher knowledge. There is also a little energetic congestion here, so it may be a good idea to double-check information coming though.

There is a clear, direct path upwards for you if you keep this awareness in your mind.

CHAPTER FIFTY-ONE

"The Death of Me" performed by City and Colour

If this is your favorite song, then you are probably special in these ways:

- Soft
- Gentle
- A deep thinker
- Pensive
- Spiritual
- Intelligence
- Appreciate poetry
- Attractive
- A secret rebel
- Enjoy interesting conversations where you can learn and grow

Client: Paul

It has been a pleasure to intuit this Song Read for you. I had not heard this music before.

I interpret your deeper connection to this song in this way:

You are a wonderful soul. You have a big energy field and there is a 'rolling' quality to you. Similar to a stone which rolls but gathers no moss.

The guitar sound represents momentum. You have a reoccurring thought that there is a momentum and progression in life. You think that life will keep moving and going on and it is our job to change because life is going to move. There is a rolling quality and a momentum quality for you. This is a helpful understanding and you can call on this understanding when you need guidance.

You are a soft, gentle soul and you are a deep thinker. You are pensive. This song connects you with Source. You are a spiritual person. You may at times have difficulty expressing your emotions. However, you have the capacity to easily overcome this.

Clairvoyantly, there is a delightful imagery of the musical instruments undertaking a journey, which once again returns to this theme of momentum. The journey of life is the underlying theme for you in song.

It's possible that the lyrics are autobiographical for you but I don't think this is the case. Your intelligence enjoys the lyrics. You may suffer from migraines at times.

The music suits you well and the sound of the singer's voice suits you well. You enjoy and appreciate the poetry and the message of the lyrics. You express as a soft, gentle Soul, who at times may over think subjects. You have a penetrating intelligence and possess penetrating thought patterns. You probably enjoy getting to the bottom of things and understanding complex issues.

You are an attractive guy.

There is gentleness in you and also a secret rebel lies hidden within you. You possibly tend to operate from your head space and you enjoy interesting conversations where you can learn and grow and share your knowledge.

Client Feedback

"Nice work Awen! How do you work this out? A great gift! You're doing a good job"

-Paul.

CHAPTER FIFTY-TWO

"The Shadow" performed by Richie Kotzen

If this is your favorite song, then you are probably special in these ways:

- Deep and mysterious
- A lover
- Think deeply
- At home in your emotions
- Have a good sense of humor
- Have a deep, beautiful smile
- Sincere
- Possess an underlying sense of faith
- Forgiving
- Appreciative and grateful
- Peaceful and content
- At home expressing love
- Easy going and popular
- Drawn to the underlying meaning in life
- Possess good morals
- Fulfil your duties easily
- Possess a strong audio faculty
- Make considered, wise choices

Client: Joshua

It has been a pleasure to intuit this Song Read for you. I had not heard this music before.

I interpret your deeper connection to this song in this way:

The sound of the guitar strings is beautiful for you. The deep connection held within this song for you is the concept of deeper meaning and hidden purposefulness.

You are deep and mysterious. You are a lover. You think deeply and you are happy for your emotions to be expressed. You are at home in your emotions and you feel alive expressing your emotions.

You are beautifully connected to Source with this song. You love the sound of this music and you like the sound of the singer's voice.

You have a good sense of humor. You have a deep, beautiful smile, which lights up through your eyes and heart. You have a sincere, deep smile.

You have an underlying sense of faith or an underlying sense of a deeper meaning revolving around you. This seems to be just on the edge of your consciousness.

Clairvoyantly, your energy field has become pink. Pink is the color of the heart chakra. You express the qualities of the heart chakra; love, forgiveness, appreciation, gratitude happiness, peace and contentment. You are at home expressing love.

You present as an easy going, popular guy. You are secretly pulled, and perhaps don't discuss this with your friends, to the underlying meaning in life. This is fun for you and this may be an area which you discover and study later in life.

There is a state of perfectness for you which you are able to arrive at. This could be a perfect day or perhaps a perfect hour, but you are conscious when you arrive at your qualification of perfection.

You truly do have a lovely wide smile. This is a beautiful quality in you.

You are sincere. You possess good morals and fulfil your duties easily.

Any career or hobby in the arts; dance, music, visual art, drama, language etc. will suit you because these disciplines allow you to express your emotions, which makes you feel alive.

You like the quality of sound. Through sound you can hook into your emotions quickly. You possess a strong audio faculty.

You have the capacity to enjoy a lot of happiness and to make considered, wise choices.

Client Feedback

"Hey Awen...

First of all, I'd like to say thank you for taking the time to not only source/locate the music in question, but also for your analysis of the piece and its relation, if any, to myself!

Being that the analysis was quite favorable/flattering - it's not likely that I'm going to reject your summary, right?! But, I have to say, you DID hit the nail on the head quite a few times... It's hardly cheating now that you've already provided your analysis, but just for you own satisfaction, I can confirm a few things that you have mentioned, if you're interested!

Now, for starters, I should point out that I find it EXTREMELY difficult to actually pick "a favorite song," and usually can't even pick a favorite artist/band, let alone a song! But, so saying, I REALLY wanted to hear what you had to say, and so, the song I picked is one I have always loved, and every time I hear it, it does something for me. I'm playing it as I type just to recapture what it is I like so much about this song!

1)"The sound of the guitar strings are beautiful for you. The deeper meaning and the hidden purposefulness of life seems to be the deeper meaning for you"

- You could NOT be more accurate with this statement! I am a guitar player, and I teach guitar by day, and perform at nights - It is truly what I have based my life around! The guitar IS beautiful to me, and Richie Kotzen is one of my (many) favorite guitar players - I won't bore you with why, but he is world class

at what he does, be that as a guitar player, a singer, AND a composer...

2) "You are deep and mysterious. You are a lover. You think deeply and you are happy for your emotions to be expressed. You are at home in your emotions and you feel alive expressing your emotions."

- I don't know if you follow Astrology, but I'm sure you have a basic knowledge, (if not more) of it! I am a Scorpio, and although you can't take anything about the signs as Gospel, I DO seem to exhibit traits that they attribute to Scorpio! As a result, I have often been described as Deep and Mysterious and also Secretive, haha... The fact is, I am a private person - and this is often perceived as the above! At the same time, I am very emotional, yet I will NOT always give away what I am thinking/feeling - and have also been accused of having No Heart, being Cold, Heart of Stone, etc... Let's just say if I ever had an interest in playing Poker (I don't!), I would probably be OK at it!

NOW - as an almost contradiction, Music and guitar playing have become my public outlet for those emotions - it has been my therapy, my saviour - and what started as a hobby became my Life! Incidentally, I often wonder why there aren't more Female musicians around. My theory is, women are SO more open with their emotions as a rule than men, so why are they not expressing it through music? It seems the ratio of men to women guitar players is quite crazy - If I had to guess, it could be as nuts as 80:1 or something! (No idea, just a guess!) - Just a thought!

3) "You have a good sense of humor. You have a very deep, beautiful smile, which goes through your eyes and your heart. You have a very sincere, deep smile."

- I DO have a good sense of humor - and I blame/credit my Dad for this! (Blame him for the bad jokes I make, but credit him for everything else!)

I can't comment on my own smile, (since I don't usually see it!) but I know how it feels when I do it, and to me, that's what matters...

4) *"You seem to have some underlying sense of faith or some underlying sense of a deeper meaning revolving around you. This seems to be just on the edge of your consciousness."*

- Being brought up in a strict Catholic family, (even being coerced into being an Altar Boy at one stage), I was taught to believe in a Higher Power, most people named it "God!" I rebelled at about 11-12 against Organized Religion - I didn't like/understand the hypocrisy of the Charlie Church-Goers, and just people in general, and there were MANY aspects of religion I didn't agree with/like as well...

Also, I always had a fascination with the unknown, the paranormal, the occult, and such topics. This led me to research on such topics, and opened my mind to the possibility of being Spiritual without being Religious, and is an attitude I still harbor today.

5) *"Your energy field has become pink. Pink is the color of the heart chakra. You express the qualities of the heart chakra; love, forgiveness, appreciation, gratitude happiness, peace and contentment. You are at home expressing love."*

This one is your department - I've got nothing!

6) *"You present yourself as an easy, popular, type of guy. But you seem to be secretly pulled, and perhaps don't discuss this with your friends, to the underlying meaning in life. This may be fun for you and this may be an area which you discover and study later on in your life."*

- Easy Going - this is definitely how I think I am. I used to "sweat the small stuff," but I try to no longer do this. I don't care if I am popular or not, but I guess playing in bands seems to help in that department! The interesting thing about being a performer is onstage, I can be anyone I want to be? In one of my bands, I am more the "cool, aloof" one - in another, I am the maniacal, "in your face" crazy man! I think the important thing is that once you step OFFSTAGE, you, for want of a better phrase, "Keep it Real!"

7) *"There is a state of perfectness for you which you are able to arrive at. This could be a perfect day or perhaps a perfect hour,*

but you are conscious when you arrive at your qualification of perfection."

- To me, this would have to come back to being by myself, and getting "lost" in my music... THIS is my meditation, and I can sometimes "Zone Out" for hours, just being totally involved in whatever I am playing...

8) *"You truly do have a lovely wide smile. This is a beautiful quality in you. You are sincere. You possess good morals and fulfill your duties easily."*

- Again, thank you for the smile compliments, haha... I would have to agree, I am pretty sincere - and TRY to keep my morals/ethics most of the time!

We all slip at times, but overall, I think I am a decent person...

9) *"Any career or hobby in the arts; dance, music, visual art, drama, language etc will probably suit you because these disciplines will allow you to express your emotions, which makes you feel alive."*

- Considering my career choice, then this is probably a GOOD thing, haha...

10) *"You like the quality of sound. Through sound you can hook into your emotions very quickly. You possess a strong audio faculty."*

- I LOVE music - and yes, this is a big part of sound. I've often thought if I had to pick between losing my sight and losing my hearing - I would have to go with sight! (Although I kinda want them both!) (And yes, these are the kinds of nutty internal conversations I have with myself!)

As far as the Audio Faculty, I agree. I inherited my Mother's musical ear! I may not be the most brilliant musical technician out there - but what has taken me to this point in my career has definitely been my ear! I can hear a pitch/sound, and know exactly what it is - whether your phone rings in the key of Bb, or your car horn consist of F Major Third intervals, I can HEAR it! Now, of course, I didn't always know what I was hearing - I learned theory along the way, but the fact is, I can still hear it...

The interesting thing is, I thought it was something EVERY-BODY did at first - but I realized after a few episodes that not everyone hears/perceives things the same. And that made me draw parallels to say, the Art world, and indeed, many other worlds... The reason some people will spend thousands on a painting that I might say, "But it looks like a kindergarten kid did that, while blindfolded!" Everyone is unique...

11) "You have the capacity to enjoy a lot of happiness and to make considered, wise choices."

- It doesn't take much to make me happy - I think happiness is once again, contentness with your lot, and being able to appreciate the things in life that truly matter. This isn't money, material possessions, etc. although we ALL fall prey to the consumerism way of thinking. I know I have the capacity to make wise choices, but again, sometimes I don't always DO this!

I don't think I am an Einstein, but I don't think I am completely retarded either! Sometimes, some lures are too attractive to resist, even though common sense is telling you otherwise. In the end, you usually do what is best, but sometimes, the lesson has to be repeated to become learned, and that's just life, I guess!

Thanks so much for your interpretation of my Chosen Song, and I hope you enjoyed the tune as much as I do! You have my consent to use as little or as much of this email reply as you like, and I'd be most interested in knowing whether you in fact DO choose to use it! I want to wish you all the best, and I'll be keeping an eye out for your publications...

I apologize for any typos along the way, or any repetition of thoughts/ideas, and hope this insight helps you along your way just a little bit...

Thanks and Regards,"

Joshua

CHAPTER FIFTY-THREE

"Throw Your Arms Around Me" performed by Hunters and Collectors

If this is your favorite song, then you are probably special in these ways:

- Spiritual
- Access the bigger vision in life
- Individual
- Genuinely appreciate the unusual in life
- Measured and considered
- Joyful
- Mischievous
- Feel safe
- Content
- Possess a broad, genuine smile

Client: Chris

It has been a pleasure to intuit this Song Read for you. I had not heard this music before.

I interpret your deeper connection to this song in this way:

There is a 'shining' element to you. This music influences and is aligned with your spirituality and your bigger vision in life. You are connected with Source with this song. The energy flows easily from above your crown, down through your body.

Your heart is full of energy. This song suits your energy well and activates your heart chakra and your crown chakra. Your higher faculties are activated. There is also a gentle aspect of mind and mental faculties present.

You are an individual character and sometimes you have a black sense of humor. You appreciate the unusual aspects and characters in life. You also enjoy unusual voices and situations. You genuinely appreciate the unusual in life.

Your temple chakras shoot open with the chorus lyrics. The temple also opens the door to higher consciousness and expanded awareness. Your energy field and the singer's voice work together very well. You like the voice of this singer. You appreciate his delivery of the words.

It's possible that you may have some issues with your sinus, pain in your nose or hay fever.

You experience life at a measured and considered pace.

This song gives you much joy. There are tears of joy. This song also helps and expands your energy field. Metaphorically, your vision is also looking upwards to The Divine. Your eyes are positioned in the upwards pose.

The rifts at the beginning of the music suggest that you are slightly mischievous. You have a mischievous quality to you and a gleam in your eyes. You show and expose yourself well through these lyrics. You feel safe. You have a wide grin. You enjoy singing along to this song, especially the chorus. There is contentment about you.

You possess a broad, genuine smile, which creates *light* in a room. Your smile reaches your eyes. You have the ability when you smile, to smile from your heart and this is a great gift.

CHAPTER FIFTY-FOUR

"Unchained Melody" performed by Righteous Brothers

If this is your favorite song, then you are probably special in these ways:

- Possess deep love and happiness
- Intuitive
- Value and possess good old fashioned, traditional virtues
- Attractive
- Romantic
- Have a good sense of humor
- Grounded to Mother earth
- Passionate
- Rational
- Practical
- Love is your truth

Client: Trudy

It has been a pleasure to intuit this Song Read for you.

I interpret the hidden messages in your favorite song and music in this way:

You possess deep happiness. Your smile is broad. There is deep love in you and you desire to express this. When you have love in your heart you symbolically float upwards. The emotion of love allows you to float. When you have deep love in your heart, you connect to others through intuition.

You are exceedingly connected to Source with this song. Your *antakarana* is developed and wide. (The Hindu Sanskrit word *antakarana* refers to the central column of energy, running through our body connecting us to The Divine and to The Earth. It is the bridge between our higher and lower consciousness.)

You value and possess good-old-fashioned, traditional virtues. You are an attractive individual and you are a romantic. You have a good sense of humor too.

You may suffer from headaches or migraines.

You are very much of the physical world and grounded to Mother earth. This music arouses passion in you. This sense of euphoric love and the way that it can symbolically raise you and allow you to float is a wonderful feeling for you.

This music allows your emotion and passions to come forward. Conversely, in life, you often operate from your rational and practical mind. You love the depth, passion and the mystery of emotions and you try to express this side of your personality to create balance.

You truly love this song. It is to your advantage to physically express your love for people more frequently, perhaps through hugging, because love is your truth. Perhaps express and show this physically to family members and friends. You'll find that you will be well received.

CHAPTER FIFTY-FIVE

"Voodoo Child" performed by Jimi Hendrix

If this is your favorite song, then you are probably special in these ways:
- Original
- Unusual
- Groovy
- Possess strong ability with detail
- Tolerant
- Patient
- Diplomatic
- Understand that there is more to life than lays on the surface
- Sexy
- Possess a natural sense of moral conscience
- Desire excitement
- Self-disciplined
- Have a wild streak
- Appreciate the creative process
- Balanced in yin and yang energy
- Interesting
- Express yourself well
- Able to make wise choices

Client: Jared

It has been a pleasure to intuit this Song Read for you. I had not heard this music before. This is an exciting song choice.

I interpret your deeper connection to the song in this way:

You are original, unusual, groovy and attuned to detail. You possess a strong affinity for detail. You have a big smile.

The message for you is: you understand that there are many pieces which make a whole. And this music is showing you the individual elements and details which go into making the whole. These details have a reason to exist and are similar to perspectives and are necessary to create a whole. You innately understand this. So this understanding will help you to be tolerant of different viewpoints, patient with other people and diplomatic.

You are nicely connected to Source. There is a strong bond.

This music gives you a sense that there is far more going on in life than is on the surface. This is connected to your sense and attunement with detail. You are interested and skilled with detail and nuances.

This music is groovy and very sexy. You are groovy and sexy too. There are secret imaginings for you, secret desires. There is a secret side to you. This is helpful in a way. It can be healthful to hold something back for yourself rather that give of your body, mind, soul and spirit. It can be helpful to keep some of your own identity.

You have a natural sense of when a situation is right and to your benefit. You also possess a natural sense of moral conscience, and this in some ways annoys you. At times you wish you didn't have this talent! This moral conscience can prevent you from having some experiences in life which you want to have. There is a dichotomy here. You find it difficult to make easy excuses for yourself, (which is to your credit.) One of the aspects which may be helpful for you to understand is that it is not necessary to be perfect in everything. There is no need to act with 100 per cent consideration with moral conscience. You are allowed to make some mistakes and you are allowed to veer off course and ease up and this may bring you great joy. The only condition is that you don't deliberately hurt people. So perhaps consider to use a sense of balance and equilibrium. Your moral conscience may hold you back at times.

You desire excitement, great sex, awesome experiences, blockbusters and mythology. You like the mythic in everything as this gives to you a sense of reason.

Also, you have a high degree of self-discipline. The 'Father' (archetype) parent is in you. 'The Father' is the parent who puts boundaries, protection and self-disciple into place. At times you may feel restricted with this, because this aspect of fathering yourself means that the times of excess and addiction don't happen for you. You tend to hold yourself in moderation and check because you have been brought up to do this. Remember, that this on the whole is helpful, but a secret desire of yours is to lose yourself.

If you can trust and converse with important people in your life about your need for more adventure and more experimentation and to bring your authenticity to the conversation and allow others to bring along their authenticity, it may well be possible for you to arrive at more opportunities for these desires of adventure and experimentation. This is within you. It may be possible that if you do not take or accept the high level of desire in these realms, you may run the risk of smothering yourself with internal resentment. So, by all means keep and adhere to your moral compass and your moral code, but also in a safe environment, perhaps consider risking bringing out your inner child, who is another side of you, who desires wildness.

This safe expression of wildness may bring you great joy. Wildness does not always involve addictions and self-centeredness. It is often taking a risk and doing something unknown and seizing these opportunities. To be clear, you already have a wild streak; you just want to be wilder.

You possess a nice wide smile and you know how to join in with the fun. You understand how to join in and be part of the group.

You have an appreciation and interest for the creative process. You are accepting and tolerant of these qualities in people. You do not expect all others to be like you.

You present as balanced in yin and yang energy—*Yin* being the feminine energy and *yang* representing the masculine energy. You are open to your emotions though you are more inclined to the intellectual and rational realm. It is possible that something has happened emotionally in your past, which may at times hold you back. This is not a severe handicap it is a moderate event which niggles you. Perhaps consider to forgive this event and move on.

This is an interesting song choice for you because it is almost unexpected. You are an interesting individual. I can see why you love this song. The guitar is so fantastic. This sound creates for you a wide energy field, potential, a sense of communion with higher self, expression, excitement, sex appeal, sex drive, attraction, magnetism, high passion and a secret desire to take risks. These are all qualities in you. This is why you like Jimi Hendrix and his guitar and this song.

You express yourself well. It may be that there is more risk taking you may wish to employ. If you choose to be safe and to not harm others and make wise choices, this will be enriching for you. You are able to make wise choices.

CHAPTER FIFTY-SIX

"Zzyzx Road" performed by Stone Sour

If this is your favorite song, then you are probably special in these ways:

- Appreciate beauty
- Romantic
- Think and feel deeply
- An open person
- Peace loving
- Sincere
- In touch with both your masculine and feminine sides.
- Heartfelt
- Imaginative
- Understand that life is a journey
- Gentle
- Intelligent
- Possess internal balance
- Open to new stimuli
- There is excitement in you

Client: Bryn

I have thoroughly enjoyed intuiting this Song Read for you. I had not heard this song before. I interpret your deeper connection to this song in this way:

You like beauty. You like and appreciate internal beauty and also external beauty. You are able to see beauty in music, beauty in aesthetics, beauty in emotion, beauty in thoughts, and beauty in synchronicity. This is an important facet of you, a natural appreciation of beauty.

You are romantic. You think and feel deeply. You are an open person. You show yourself to others, which is healthy. You do not tend to hide yourself behind masks.

There is a gentle peace loving quality to you. You are sincere. Your heart is open and you are open to your friends, family and to love. You are in touch with both your masculine and feminine sides.

Your energy field is nice and clean and open. Very little will hold you back in life. You are able to go through life in a healthful and helpful way. You do not tend to get bound up in a lot of unnecessary worries and complications. Possibly, at times you feel confused, but you have within you the power to arrive at satisfactory, effective, flexible and sustainable solutions. If necessary remember to take extra time when confusing situations present themselves.

The piano music easily connects you to Source and of all the musical instruments, the piano stands out for you. You like the other instruments too. You like the deep feeling and the emotional depths, the sincerity and the heartfelt aspects, which are expressed in this music. These qualities are in you too.

Music suits you and works well with you. When you are listening to music, without accompanying lyrics, you are able to see, feel and comprehend the beauty of the different instruments working together. Your imagination kicks in and you feel a sense of aliveness.

Combining your natural strengths of appreciation of beauty with your imaginative capabilities allows you to arrive at a sense of deep love.

This song is great for you and opens up your upper chakras, although all of your chakras are strong and healthy. This music opens up the higher chakras in your energy body, so symbolically, you are looking upwards to The Divine. The music also opens up chakras from your shoulders. There is a clairvoyant image of a parachute, and possibly this pulls you up to The Divine.

The keys on the piano represent the path of life. The skipping, hopping and jumping over keys and progressing through keys. The piano keys symbolise the element of a journey.

Your energy body fills with energy when you listen to this music. You become very alive. This indicates that this is a wonderful choice of song for you.

You are gentle and intelligent. You are aware of difficulties and challenges and the options these challenges present, but because of your internal balance and openness to new stimuli you are able to carve a path through life. This is a wonderful ability, to clear the path so that you can progress forward. So ultimately this song brings you to the excitement of the future and the excitement in you.

Returning to the piano. The piano keys are black and white, yin and yang, masculine and feminine. They can symbolise opposites. The law of polarity exists here on planet earth. You have an understanding that this law of polarity exists and you are able to choose wisely and with consideration of this polarity.

The piano keys are a strong image for you and the sound of the piano is too. It is an image which is within you.

You will enjoy the definition of beauty from The Collins Australian Dictionary: "the combination of all the qualities of a person or thing that delight the senses and mind."

ABOUT THE AUTHOR

AWEN FINN

About the Author

Awen Finn, who has been described as having a mix of Tina Turner's energy, Stevie Nicks' brilliance and Ella Fitzgerald's range, was born in the United Kingdom and began her career in fashion before moving to Australia. In Sydney, Awen went on to develop a successful business in the art world, co-founding art galleries and a successful art publishing company.

Awen began her journey in spirituality after attending a meditation class with a friend. She went on to train and qualify as an energy healer and spiritual teacher before she began to understand the incredible connection hidden within music and the spiritual energy of the world. She now interprets how to apply this life-changing knowledge in people's favorite songs while completely transforming their understanding of music and its energy.

Read other Books by this Author:
Read My Song, Read My Heart, Read My Soul
How to Beat Criticism and Feel Good.

Acknowledgments

My deepest thanks to my first spiritual teachers, my parents Frances and Thomas, and for all they've given me.

My very special thanks to my partner, my son and my daughter for bringing love, laughter and joy to my life. Thank you Dave for your continual support and encouragement. Thank you for always being there to cheer me on! Thank you Jens for your valuable help and assistance with my earliest writing efforts and for gifting me with the confidence to express Song Reads.

My special thanks to Paramahansa Yogananda and Sri Yukteswar. An enormous thank you for your teaching, guidance and for accompanying me on this journey.

Thank you to The Divine for working through me.

I have a special gratitude in my heart for all of the wonderful song writers, composers and musicians whose songs are referred to in these pages. I am in awe at your talents-truly in awe. Thank you.

I'd like to thank Mike Scott and The Waterboys for composing my own favorite song, "This is The Sea."

And most of all, I would like to thank all of the many people who contributed their favorite songs to the pages of this book. Without the help of these individuals, who so generously shared their favorite songs, this book could never have been written. Their support for my efforts means more to me than I can express.

Contact Awen

To get the latest updates and resources visit:

readmysongreadmysoul.com

Awen speaks frequently on the topic of Song Reads.™ She can deliver a keynote, half-day, or full-day version of this content, depending on your needs. If you are interested in finding out more, please visit her contact page at:

readmysongreadmysoul.com/contact

You can also connect with Awen here:
Blog: *www.readmysongreadmysoul.com*
Twitter: *twitter.com/ReadmySong*
Facebook: *facebook.com/pages/Read-My-Song-Read-My-Soul/1439109376353372*
Pinterest: *pinterest.com/ReadmySong*
Instagram: *instagram.com/readmysong*

THANK YOU

You've finished the book but there's much more waiting for you online!

FREE CHAPTERS
COMPETITIONS
FREE RESOURCES

So go ahead now and visit the link below to access all of your resources

http://readmysongreadmysoul.com

INTRODUCING
MY NEW ETSY SHOP

Soul Music inspirational cards and art prints for musicians and the special musician and music lover in your life

100 BEST MUSIC QUOTES for daily inspiration

Visit   www.etsy.com/shop/ReadMySongReadMySoul

Surround yourself with beauty and positive inspirational words and notice how good you feel

Now that you have finished reading the book
I'd love for you to leave a review on Amazon. It would mean the world to me.
Many thanks and Blessings

Have you ever wondered what your favorite song says about you?

Deep inside your favorite song lay the secret messages that unlock your psyche and all your potential. Song Reads are an awesome and fascinating way to discover your personality type so YOU can lead a life of happiness and success

Sign up here to stay in the loop and to be the first to receive hot off the press notifications about new releases from Awen Finn and Read My Song, Read My Soul

Sign up here
http://readmysongreadmysoul.com

www.ingramcontent.com/pod-product-compliance
Lightning Source LLC
LaVergne TN
LVHW051548070426
835507LV00021B/2465